First World War
and Army of Occupation
War Diary
France, Belgium and Germany

7 INDIAN (MEERUT) DIVISION
Headquarters, Branches and Services
Commander Royal Artillery
1 March 1915 - 31 March 1915

WO95/3933/3

The Naval & Military Press Ltd
www.nmarchive.com
Published in association with The National Archives

Published by

The Naval & Military Press Ltd

Unit 10 Ridgewood Industrial Park,

Uckfield, East Sussex,

TN22 5QE England

Tel: +44 (0) 1825 749494

www.naval-military-press.com

www.nmarchive.com

This diary has been reprinted in facsimile from the original. Any imperfections are inevitably reproduced and the quality may fall short of modern type and cartographic standards.

© **Crown Copyright**
Images reproduced by permission of The National Archives, London, England, 2015.

Contents

Document type	Place/Title	Date From	Date To
Heading	Meerut Division H.Q.Div Artillery From 1st to 31st March 1915		
Heading	War Diary with Appendices of Head Quarters Divisional Artillery Meerut Division From 1st March 1915 To 31st March 1915		
War Diary	Locon	01/03/1915	08/03/1915
War Diary	Veille Chapelle	09/03/1915	13/03/1915
War Diary	Locon	14/03/1915	24/03/1915
War Diary	Estaires-La Bassee Road M 14.b.5.0	25/03/1915	26/03/1915
War Diary	Veille Chapelle	27/03/1915	31/03/1915
Miscellaneous	List Of Hostile Batteries Opposite Meerut Divisional Artillery With Their Target Numbers And Map Positions	03/03/1915	03/03/1915
Miscellaneous	Result Of Experiment In Lashing Wheels Carried Out By The 14th Battery Royal Field Artillery On The 4th March 1915	04/03/1915	04/03/1915
Operation(al) Order(s)	Operation Order No.21 By Lieut: General Sir Charles Anderson K.C.B. Commanding Meerut Division	09/03/1915	09/03/1915
Operation(al) Order(s)	Operation Order No.10 By Brigadier General R. St. C. Lecky R.A. Commanding Royal Artillery Meerut Divn.	09/03/1915	09/03/1915
Miscellaneous	Schedule Operation Royal Artillery-1st Phase		
Miscellaneous	Operation By Royal Artillery Meerut Division	10/03/1915	10/03/1915
Heading	War Diary Meerut D.A March 1915		
Map	Map		
Heading	War Diary Meerut D.A March 1915		
Heading	War Diary December 1914 Hd.Qs. Divisional Artillery Meerut Division		
Map	Map		
Heading	War Diary Meerut D.A March 1915		
Operation(al) Order(s)	Operation Order No.11 By Brigadier General R. St. C. Lecky R.A. Commanding Royal Artillery Meerut Divn.	11/03/1915	11/03/1915
Miscellaneous	Operation Royal Artillery Meerut Division	11/03/1915	11/03/1915
Operation(al) Order(s)	Operation Order No.12 By Brigadier General R. St. C. Lecky R.A. Commanding Royal Artillery Meerut Divn.	12/03/1915	12/03/1915
Miscellaneous	Operation Order No.12 by Brigadier General R. St. C. Lecky R.A. Commanding Royal Artillery Meerut Division	12/03/1915	12/03/1915
Miscellaneous	Operation Royal Artillery Meerut Division	12/03/1915	12/03/1915
Miscellaneous	Report By 2nd Lieutenant A.Brownlee 8th Battery R.F.A.	12/03/1915	12/03/1915
Operation(al) Order(s)	Operation Order No.22 By Lieutenant-General Sir C.A. Anderson K.C.B. Commanding Meerut Division	13/03/1915	13/03/1915
Miscellaneous	Appendix 123		
Map	Map		
Miscellaneous	Operations Royal Artillery Meerut Division	13/03/1915	13/03/1915
Miscellaneous	Method Adopted by The 4th Brigade Royal Field Artillery For Making Their Guns Fast During The Operations of The 10th March 1915	02/04/1918	02/04/1918

Miscellaneous	Report On Anchorage Of Guns And Platforms In Connection Therewith As Carried Out By Batteries Of 9th Brigade Royal Field Artillery For "Wire-Cutting" On 10th March 1915	01/04/1915	01/04/1915
Miscellaneous	The Following Method Of Anchoring Guns Was Adopted By The 13th Brigade Royal Field Artillery During The "Wire Cutting" Operations On The 10th March 1915	02/04/1915	02/04/1915
Miscellaneous	A Form Messages And Signals		
Miscellaneous	The 4th & 13th Bde will be arm issuing orders		
Miscellaneous	A Form Messages And Signals		
Miscellaneous	Messages And Signals		
Miscellaneous	A Form Messages And Signals		
Miscellaneous	Intelligence Summary	01/03/1915	01/03/1915
Miscellaneous	Intelligence Summary	02/03/1915	02/03/1915
Miscellaneous	Intelligence Summary	03/03/1915	03/03/1915
Miscellaneous	Intelligence Summary	04/03/1915	04/03/1915
Miscellaneous	Intelligence Summary	05/03/1918	05/03/1918
Miscellaneous	Intelligence Summary	06/03/1915	06/03/1915
Miscellaneous	Intelligence Summary	07/03/1915	07/03/1915
Miscellaneous	Intelligence Summary	08/03/1915	08/03/1915
Miscellaneous	Time Table First Phase		
Miscellaneous	Second Phase		
Miscellaneous	Ammunition Expended On 10th, 11th, 12th and 13th March 1915 By Lahore and Meerut Divsnl Artillery	13/03/1915	13/03/1915
Heading	Meerut Div C.R.A. March 1915		

Meerut Division

H.Q. Div. Artillery

From 1st to 31st March 1915

121/5114

WAR DIARY

With Appendices.

Head Quarters, Divisional Artillery, Meerut Division.

From 1st March 1915 to 31st March 1915

Army Form C. 2118.

WAR DIARY VOLUME VIII
OF
INTELLIGENCE SUMMARY.
(Erase heading not required.)

Hour, Date, Place	Summary of Events and Information	Remarks and references to Appendices
7 a.m. 1st March 1915. LOCON	114th Battery fired at barricade in S.5.c - relief entering fire trench without rifles	
7.30. a.m. do	73rd Battery fired a few rounds at Breastwork in front of PICQUET House where new work had been done - Enemy's cook fire put out	
8.30. a.m. do	FORT ARTHUR shelled by hostile battery, which stopped when 19th Battery R.F.A opened with gun fire	
9.25. a.m. do	46 now active - 110th Heavy Battery fired 2 rounds at him and he shut up at once -	× Appendix 111
10. a.m. do	2 of our 2 enemy guns located by flashes in S.18.c and ranged on by 66th Battery R.F.A.	
10.30. a.m. do	114th Battery fired at snipers in fire trench S.10.6.9.9.	
10.45. a.m. do	8th Siege Battery engaged hostile battery at S.18.a.4.1.	× Appendix 123
11.15. a.m. do	observation post of 30th How Battery shelled by enemy's light howitzer, and again at 1.30.p.m and 3.30.p.m - No damage done -	
11.20. a.m. do	8th Siege Battery again engaged hostile battery at S.18.a.4.1 with observation from RUE du BOIS and obtained direct hit - the observing officer reporting that fragments of material flew in all directions -	
11.25. a.m. do	2nd Siege registered on WHITE House with 5 rounds heavy lyddite - 1 direct hit	
12.1. p.m. do	114th Battery R.F.A. shelled M.G. parapet at S.10.d.7.4 - last round hit top of parapet.	
12.30. p.m. do	RITZ shelled - thought to be by 527 - and again at 3.20.p.m	
12.45. p.m. do	8th Siege Battery engaged hostile battery at S.18.d.7.1 with observation from RUE du BOIS. the point which its flashes had been observed was successfully swept.	

WAR DIARY
or
INTELLIGENCE SUMMARY.
(Erase heading not required.)

Army Form C. 2118.

Instructions regarding War Diaries and Intelligence Summaries are contained in F.S. Regs., Part II. and the Staff Manual respectively. Title pages will be prepared in manuscript.

Hour, Date, Place	Summary of Events and Information	Remarks and references to Appendices
1.20.p.m. 1st March 1915 LOCON	2nd Siege Battery registered on DISTILLERY with 7 rounds heavy lyddite – 3 direct hits –	+ Appendix III
1.55 p.m. do.	2nd Siege Battery registered on LITTLE GREY HOME (S.17.d.0.0) with 6 rounds heavy lyddite.	
About 2.p.m. do.	Iron plates thought to be M.G. shields were seen in pairs at two places one in the trench S.10.c. and one in support trench S.10.T. 7.2. – latter enfilading our front as far as CINDER TRACK – 66th Battery then put 10 more rounds into Redoubt where there was movement.	
2.20.p.m. do.	2nd Siege Battery registered with 4 rounds light lyddite on hedge W of VIOLAINES Brewery where 73rd Battery saw flashes of heavy hostiles yesterday.	+ App. Nos 1 2 3
2.45.p.m. do.	Reported by O.C. 2nd Siege Battery that hostile battery in S.28 b.3.4. opened fire – 2 guns distinctly located – engaged and silenced by 35th Heavy Battery.	
3.p.m. do.	14th Battery R.F.A. fired at party carrying sacks in communication trench S.5.c. 4 hostile field guns opened fire from RUE du MARAIS at our front but without effect. No 5 Very active – 2nd Siege unable to engage it owing to heavy Snow storm.	
3.30.p.m do.	One gun of hostile battery at S.28 & 4.3 again opened fire – one gun 2/Siege – 35th Heavy Battery and 73rd Battery R.F.A. cooperated with good effect.	
4.35.p.m. do.	2nd Siege Battery registered Target No 3 with 8 rds high lyddite – appearing effective.	

Army Form C. 2118.

WAR DIARY
or
INTELLIGENCE SUMMARY.
(Erase heading not required.)

Instructions regarding War Diaries and Intelligence Summaries are contained in F.S. Regs., Part II. and the Staff Manual respectively. Title pages will be prepared in manuscript.

Hour, Date, Place	Summary of Events and Information	Remarks and references to Appendices
5.45.pm 1st March 1915. LOCON	66th Battery fired 3 rounds at a M.G. emplacement in German trenches.	SM.2.S.
7.15.pm do	14th Battery R.F.A. fired 2 rounds at M.G's in S.10.d which were annoying our Infantry in Richbourg - one round reported as effective - M.G.'s stopped firing.	
2.a.m 2nd March 1915. LOCON	66th Battery shelled party of 40 to 50 German Infantry repairing parapet and stopped work for the night.	
6.45 a.m do	14th Battery fired two salvos at Germans in Richbourg Redoubt.	
7.a.m do	14th Battery fired on relief parties in barricade S.5.c	
8.30 a.m do	14th Battery registered barricade where enemy's fire trench crossed LA BASSEE road in S.10.T.	×appendix 123
8.45 a.m do	8th Siege Battery registered with aerial observation on NEUVE CHAPELLE and set fire to a house at the cross-roads at the 64th round.	
9.a.m do	14th Battery registered fire trench where it crossed cinder track in S.10.T.	
9.30 a.m do	14th Battery registered PINK House at W corner of BOIS du BIEZ in S.5.d.	
10.30 a.m do	2nd Siege & 4.7 Battery reported field guns in S.25.b.3.4 opened as normal towards BREWERY. Observation Officers and Siege Battery fired a section of 35th Heavy Battery on to them and silenced them after 3 rounds. Observing Officers also reports he could actually see the firing number full the lanyard. 30th How. Battery O.P. RUE du BOIS - RUE du BOIS shelled - also at 2.30 p.m shells fell to right and left of it.	×Appendix III
11.a.m do	66th Battery shelled Redoubt in S.10 with aeroplane observation - Results very poor - Hashes observed from RITZ salient factory - 12 rounds were fired - 4 were target and remainder 2nd Siege Battery fired at house in S.62.9.9. with wireless aeroplane observation target unobserved - 2 rounds fired with 2nd round the shrapnel on to PIETRE cross roads - both unobserved -	

Army Form C. 2118.

WAR DIARY
or
INTELLIGENCE SUMMARY.
(Erase heading not required.)

Instructions regarding War Diaries and Intelligence Summaries are contained in F.S. Regs., Part II. and the Staff Manual respectively. Title pages will be prepared in manuscript.

Hour, Date, Place	Summary of Events and Information	Remarks and references to Appendices
11.15 a.m. 2nd March 1915. LOCON	8th Siege Battery engaged active hostile battery located by photos at S.30.c.2.9. which is a house. Roof of this house was removed and six rounds were estimated as falling in the approximate position of the battery - observation from RITZ.	
12.10 p.m. do	RITZ shelled by field battery from direction of LORGIES, but flashes could not be located. Again shelled at 2.25 p.m. and 4.30 p.m.	
2.20 p.m. do	O/C 110th Heavy Battery reported that Red Coon Wagon team on LORGIES BEAU PUITS Road - probably picked up caounal ties of No. 5. *	*Appendix III
3. p.m. do	2nd Battery R.F.A. fired ten rounds at School House, where another M.G. was reported to be.	
3.10 p.m. do	14th Battery fired a few rounds at party of Germans walking in communication trench.	
3.20. do / 3.45 p.m. do	14th Battery fired on snipers in pig net post S.10.8.	x Appendix 123
3.30 p.m. do	8th Siege Battery obtained short bracket on battery at T.19a.1.3 with aerial observation.	
4.30 p.m. do	66th Battery shelled likely house (observing) and 4 direct hits were obtained.	
4.50 p.m. do	14th Battery negro trench probable O.P. in S.5.C.5.2 Infantry reported it as being occupied by enemy.	
6.30 p.m. do	14th Battery fired 3 rounds at trench gun in enemy fire trench. Whilst on Sanfairs bent returned. Daily Intelligence summary attacked.	M.M.G.

Army Form C. 2118.

WAR DIARY
or
INTELLIGENCE SUMMARY.
(Erase heading not required.)

Instructions regarding War Diaries and Intelligence Summaries are contained in F.S. Regs., Part II. and the Staff Manual respectively. Title pages will be prepared in manuscript.

Hour, Date, Place	Summary of Events and Information	Remarks and references to Appendices
7.35 a.m. 3rd February 1915. LOCON	114th Battery obtained direct hit on house in S.5.d from which smoke and men were seen to issue.	
8.35 a.m. do	114th Battery fired on parties of enemy proceeding down communication trench in S.5.c.	
11.30 a.m. do	Enemy battery shelled RICHEBOURG 3rd MAST - battery not located.	
11.40 a.m. do	O.C. 110 Heavy Battery reported No 46 active. 114th Battery fired on house on LA BASSEE - ESTAIRES road in S.10.b, reported by our Infantry in PORT ARTHUR as probable O.P.	*Appendix 111
12. noon do	2nd Siege Battery registered on WHITE House and DISTILLERY.	
1.35 p.m. do	114th Battery fired at snipers in S.10.b with poor effect.	
1.40 p.m. do	No 5 active. - reported by 110th Heavy Battery.	
3. p.m. do	RITZ shelled - thought to be by 52.b. and again at 3.40 p.m.	*appendix 123
3 to 3.30 p.m. do	PIPSQUEAK shelled O.P. of 30th Hon. Battery - all shell about 150 short. Enemy battery shelled observation post of 114th Battery which fired at Battery in S.17.b.	
3.15 p.m. do	114th Battery fired on snipers in trench in S.5.c.	
3.25 p.m. do	2nd Siege Battery bombarded Redoubt at S.10 & 5.9 - part of parapet to left and rear of it blown away.	
3.33 p.m. do	116th Battery fired at Redoubt in cooperation with 2nd Siege.	
5. p.m. do	114th Battery fired on Germans carrying planks in communication trench S.5.c.	
8.45 p.m. do	66th Battery R.F.A. fired bursts on trenches between Redoubt and Cinder Track to stop bursts of fire from German trenches. List of targets attached. MEERUT Divisional Artillery on 3rd March 1915. Daily Intelligence Summary attached.	VW3 *appendix 111

WAR DIARY
or
INTELLIGENCE SUMMARY.
(Erase heading not required.)

Army Form C. 2118.

Instructions regarding War Diaries and Intelligence Summaries are contained in F.S. Regs., Part II. and the Staff Manual respectively. Title pages will be prepared in manuscript.

Hour, Date, Place	Summary of Events and Information	Remarks and references to Appendices
4th March 1915 LOCON	There was a very marked increase of activity on the part of the hostile artillery which was almost entirely confined to that howitzers. Their objective apparently being the houses along the RUE du BOIS between the cross roads S.9.d.1.7 and S.10.c.9.9.	
7.20 a.m. do	66th Battery fired a few rounds at Redoubt which Germans were repairing.	
7.30 a.m. do	German "Sausage" seen about 15,000° S.S.E. of LA COUTURE - descended at 2.p.m	x Appendix III
8.30 to 9 a.m. do	Road between WINDY CORNER and RUE du BOIS shelled by a howitzer and field battery - though to be 5 and 52 respectively.	
8.45 a.m. do	14th Battery fired 5 rounds on party carrying sandbags in communication trench and Redoubt S.10.T.6.2.	x Appendix 123
9 a.m. do	7th Battery fired 6 rounds on German trenches where enemy were observed to be active.	
10.a.m. do	RUE du BOIS shelled rather more heavily than usual - Besides usual PIPSQUEAK a large H.E. shell was used and, judged by fuze picked up, is a 12 c.m. Howitzer. 14th Battery fired 4 rounds at snipers firing at our aeroplane at trench S.4.d.8.2. Two dark grey uniforms seen here with peaked cap - black peak. 2nd German "Sausage" seen at quite close to one which was reported at 10.a.m - this one also descended at 2.p.m.	
10.5 a.m. do	RUE du BOIS shelled by howitzer battery - not located.	
11.15 a.m. do	Lt. 14th Battery carried out experiment of flashed shield and trail fixed - on which he submitted a report.	g appendix III A
11.45 a.m. do	RITZ and RUE du BOIS shelled by hostile howitzer battery (15 c.m.) direction apparent 130° True - this was refired at 3.50 and 5. p.m.	
12.25 p.m. do	RUE du BOIS shelled by howitzer battery - possibly 18 (T.19.T).	
12.35 p.M. do	7th Battery fired a few rounds on Snipers House S.4.T.6.4.	
12.40. p.m. do	7th Battery fired a few rounds on German Archie Gun in trench S.4T.57 - appeared effective.	

Army Form C. 2118.

WAR DIARY
or
INTELLIGENCE SUMMARY.
(Erase heading not required.)

Instructions regarding War Diaries and Intelligence Summaries are contained in F. S. Regs., Part II. and the Staff Manual respectively. Title pages will be prepared in manuscript.

Hour, Date, Place	Summary of Events and Information	Remarks and references to Appendices
4th March 1915 LOCON	O.C. 110th Heavy Battery reported 46 as active – this was also reported by O.C. 2nd Siege Battery.	x Appendix 111
1. p.m	146th Battery fired on parties entering fire trench from Redoubt S10 b.	x Appendix 123
1.30. p.m do	PORT ARTHUR shelled – one section of 146th Battery replied by firing 4 rounds at B6 – S17a, and 2 rounds at Distillery S17a – the shelling of PORT ARTHUR then ceased.	MR9
3.20. p.m do	RVE An BOIS shelled by Howitzer battery – not located.	
4.30. p.m do	Daily Intelligence Summary attached	

Army Form C. 2118.

WAR DIARY
or
INTELLIGENCE SUMMARY.
(Erase heading not required.)

Instructions regarding War Diaries and Intelligence Summaries are contained in F.S. Regs., Part II. and the Staff Manual respectively. Title pages will be prepared in manuscript.

Hour, Date, Place	Summary of Events and Information	Remarks and references to Appendices
5th March 1915. LOCON	On the whole the enemy's artillery was not so active along the RUE du BOIS today.	
12.30 p.m. do	66th Battery opened fire on observation house at S.10.d.9.6 - This house seemed to be the O.P. for "PIPSQUEAK" Battery	
1.10 p.m. do	66th Battery fired 4 rounds on working party in Redoubt S.10.a. - Also fired 2 rounds at this target at 5.p.m.	
2 p.m. do	2nd Battery registered RED House Farm S.16.d.O.O.	
2.15 p.m. do	Enemy PIPSQUEAK shelled Sahurin in N.4.J.2.2 - 7th Battery R.F.A. replied by shelling enemy's trenches - fire appeared very effective.	× Appendix 123
2.30 p.m. do	14th Battery shelled ruined house in S.17.a.5.6 as Infantry reported enemy's observer there - this house was shelled whenever German Howitzers opened fire.	
3.30 p.m. do	German battery from direction of NEUVE CHAPELLE shelled RICHEBOURG St VAAST - 7th Battery replied by shelling enemy trenches.	
6 p.m. do	14th Battery fired several effective rounds on party of about 60 Germans leaving the trench via Redoubt S.10.G.	
8 p.m. do	66th Battery fired and stopped enemy's machine gun. 30th Howitzer Battery carried out registration during the day. Daily Intelligence summary attached.	WR

Army Form C. 2118.

WAR DIARY
or
INTELLIGENCE SUMMARY.
(Erase heading not required.)

Instructions regarding War Diaries and Intelligence Summaries are contained in F. S. Regs., Part II, and the Staff Manual respectively. Title pages will be prepared in manuscript.

Hour, Date, Place.	Summary of Events and Information.	Remarks and references to Appendices
7.a.m 6th March 1915. LOCON	114th Heavy Battery registered on NEUVE CHAPPELLE	
10 a.m — do —	2nd Siege Battery registered 3 guns on barricade in S.10.b.87 - 30 yards of parapet destroyed.	
10.25 a.m — do —	Lt. 110th Heavy Battery reported 4b active.	
10.50 a.m — do —	Enemy battery shelled the RITZ at 2.45 p.m - firing on Red Observation Horse - stopped him every time.	× Appendix 111
11 a.m to 11.30 a.m — do —	Enemy's batteries strenuous shell very near O.P. - field + howitzer - 114th Battery fired 10 rounds into probable O.P. in S.17a and destroying behind - one turret in window of O.P.	× Appendix 123
2.15 p.m — do —	2nd Battery engaged Distillery - few rounds also fired on road to South.	
2.30 to 3 p.m — do —	Heavy bombard of O.P. 2nd Battery in RUE du BOIS (S.14 & 10.9) shelled by enemy.	
2.40 p.m — do —	66th Battery shelled likely O.P. of PIPSQUEAK who was firing at RITZ	
3.15 p.m — do —	2/ Siege Battery partially registered on various points about corner of S.4 a, b, c + d.	
4 p.m — do —	2/ Siege Battery partially registered on S.4 & H.3 - horses in Redoubt. Daily Artillery summary attached	WRJ

Army Form C. 2118.

WAR DIARY
or
INTELLIGENCE SUMMARY.
(Erase heading not required.)

Instructions regarding War Diaries and Intelligence Summaries are contained in F. S. Regs., Part II, and the Staff Manual respectively. Title pages will be prepared in manuscript.

Hour, Date, Place.	Summary of Events and Information.	Remarks and references to Appendices
7.15 am 7th March 1915. LOCON	30th How Battery registered on Redoubt in S.10 & 6.1.	
8 a.m. do	14th Battery R.F.A. fired 4 rounds on party of men carrying sacks for communication to the trench.	
8.35 a.m. do	14th Battery fired 4 rounds at snipers in post at S.5.C.	
9.50 a.m. do	7th Battery reported PIPSQUEAK fired on road in S.38.	
10 a.m. do	Observing station of 30th How Battery shelled with PIPSQUEAKS - no damage done.	
11.15 a.m. do	110th Heavy Battery registered on battery in S.17.a.6.4. ×	× Appendix 111
	O.C. 110th Heavy Battery reported S.2 active. 110th Heavy Battery fired a few × rounds at him. 110th Heavy Battery also fired on hostile party near DISTILLERY - who stopped very promptly and party disappeared.	
12.30 p.m. do	7th Battery reported considerable activity near house M.34.d.9.5 - apparently working party - turned wire entanglement just in front of this house.	× Appendix 123
1.30 p.m. do	14th Battery fired 4 rounds on house at corner of road S.11.a which was set on fire by 30th How Battery.	
2. p.m. do	RITZ shelled - probably by 52.? ×	
2.45 p.m. do	110th Heavy Battery ranged on RED OBSERVATION HOUSE with time shrapnel. Second salvo effective.	
2.50 p.m. do	46 active and fired on by 110th Heavy Battery with 6.5a huge - seemed to effective.	
3.30 p.m. do	110th Heavy Battery fired at various of the first houses near PORT ARTHUR with a low fuze and got good effect on them.	
3.57 p.m. do	A "PIPSQUEAK" Battery fired anchor U BOIS du BIEZ shelled angle of roads S.2.7.9.9. ×	
4.10 p.m. do	110th Heavy Battery reported 5" no active firing 4 guns with salvos.	

Army Form C. 2118.

WAR DIARY
or
INTELLIGENCE SUMMARY.
(Erase heading not required.)

Instructions regarding War Diaries and Intelligence Summaries are contained in F. S. Regs., Part II, and the Staff Manual respectively. Title pages will be prepared in manuscript.

Hour, Date, Place.	Summary of Events and Information.	Remarks and references to Appendices
8th March 1915 LOCON	Strong gusty wind made accurate shoots impossible.	
6.35 am	114th Battery fired at party carrying sandbags in S10b.	
9.30 am	114th Battery registered portion of trench in S10b to avoid disturbing working party tonight.	
10.10 am	114th Heavy Battery commenced firing with aeroplane observation on targets F and G – after 2 rounds wireless apparatus got out of order –	
10.50 am	114th Battery registered communication trench in S5c.	
12.40 PM	At 110th Heavy Battery reported 5·2 shelling the RITZ – 5·2 also fired a few rounds at 3 PM.	
1 PM	114th Heavy Battery recommenced firing on targets F & G with aeroplane observation – wireless unsatisfactory.	✗ Appendix 111
4 PM	PIPSQUEAK shelled 96 Piccadilly with 10 rounds – 30f which grazed roof of 30th Battery billet – no damage done. Lt 110th Heavy Battery reported that 46* fired 3 rounds – 110th H.B. fired time shrapnel at RED OBSERVATION House – but unfortunately telephone broke down when 46 fired and by the time it was right again, 46 was quiet. During the day Lewburg Battery shelled turns in S5c* S·2 and S11c* 9·8 am trenches in S4b. Registration very difficult owing to high winds. 66th Battery registered parts of trenches	✗ appendix 123
	Daily Intelligence Summary attached.	WRG

Army Form C. 2118.

WAR DIARY
or
INTELLIGENCE SUMMARY.
(Erase heading not required.)

Instructions regarding War Diaries and Intelligence Summaries are contained in F. S. Regs., Part II, and the Staff Manual respectively. Title pages will be prepared in manuscript.

Hour, Date, Place.	Summary of Events and Information.	Remarks and references to Appendices
7.10 to 8.20 a.m. 9th March 1915 VIEILLE CHAPELLE	Successful registration with aeroplane observation on targets F & G carried out by 114th Heavy Battery.	
7.30 a.m. do.	14th Battery fired at working party Redoubt S.10.7. Hingerwater Bougeoise Artillery opened at Estaminet near bridge R.34.a 3.5. x	
10.30 a.m. do.	60th Battery fired on enemys trenches on our working party at S.4.a.8.9. x has been worried by snipers – snipers stopped.	
11.15 a.m. do.	114th Heavy Battery registered on M.35.c x 4.5 and cross roads S.4 & 7.4 x	* Appendix 112
2 p.m. do.	Successfully MEERUT Divnl Obsy Offr No 21 reconnoitred and verified trenches –	
2.30 p.m. do.	14th Battery fired a few rounds on enemys trenches S.10.b. x	x Appendix 123
3.45 p.m. do.	14th Battery fired on party walking behind fire trenches S.5. – Two men seen in civilian clothes near here.	x Appendix 111
do.	During the day:– 30th How Battery registered German trenches S.5. – also LA BASSEE – ESTAIRES road. S.W. corner and Redoubt S.10.7. 4.2 to N.W. Four cross roads S.17.a to N.W. 2nd Siege registered Barricade S.10 Z.7.5 (trenched). Redoubt near SIX TREES S.4.7.9.1 (trenched) cube of area 2nd Phase – Trenches S.10 Z.7.3 – cube of area 3rd Phase. (These places took place in 10th) 110th Heavy Battery registered with lyddite on 17 and 17b with aeroplane + the round might hit 17a. 110th Heavy Battery reported PIPSQUEAK (5.2) shelled RUE du BOIS and RITZ morning and afternoon – 110th in return fired at RED OBSERVATION House. 110th Heavy Battery reported 46 active in morning and fired time shrapnel at her with good effect – 110th Heavy Battery reported 5 active in morning and afternoon was engaged but when fired with lyddite effect looked good. Captured German Battery Nº 10 round by Howitzer Battery	+ Appendix 113

8. p.m.
ϕ Appendix 113

Army Form C. 2118.

WAR DIARY
or
INTELLIGENCE SUMMARY.
(Erase heading not required.)

Instructions regarding War Diaries and Intelligence Summaries are contained in F. S. Regs., Part II, and the Staff Manual respectively. Title pages will be prepared in manuscript.

Hour, Date, Place.	Summary of Events and Information.	Remarks and references to Appendices
10th March 1915. VIEILLE CHAPELLE	Majority of batteries registered the targets for their days task during the afternoon of the 9th and early morning of 10th.	
7.15 am do	O.C. 4th Bde R.F.A. reported 46* active on PORT ARTHUR – O.C. No 1 Group Heavy Artillery was asked to turn heavy batteries on and silence it.	* Appendix 111
7.30 am do	109th Heavy Battery reported through 4th Bde R.F.A. that their 'wireless' out of order. All batteries opened fire in accordance with orders for 1st Phase of [scheme of operations] (See operation order No 10 by C.R.A. of 9.3.15)	+ Appendix 113
7.49 am do	66th Battery R.F.A. reported fire very satisfactory – Locked wire being destroyed.	
8.10 am do	MEERUT Division report on wire – reported by runner that LORGIES alarm of troops. This was communicated to O.C. No 1 Group Heavy Artillery.	× Appendices 115 & 116
8.24 am do	Message received from General Staff, MEERUT Division that GARHWAL Brigade report our Infantry advance at 8.10 a.m.	
8.25 am do	66th Battery reported that GARHWALIS had captured first trench.	
8.35 am do	4th Bde R.F.A. reports BLUE flag at point 'B' 2nd Siege Battery – were asked to confirm.	×
8.45 am do	4th Bde R.F.A. reported Black Watch 50 yds N.W of point 'N'. – 14th Battery increased range by 100 yds. 14th Battery R.F.A. Observers officers reported fire trench taken as far as LA BASSÉE Road – many prisoners reported as having been seen.	

Gulab Singh & Sons, Calcutta—No. 22 Army C.—5·8·14—1,07,000.

Army Form C. 2118.

WAR DIARY
or
INTELLIGENCE SUMMARY.

(Erase heading not required.)

Instructions regarding War Diaries and Intelligence Summaries are contained in F. S. Regs., Part II, and the Staff Manual respectively. Title pages will be prepared in manuscript.

Hour, Date, Place.	Summary of Events and Information.	Remarks and references to Appendices
8.55 am. 10th March 1915. VIEILLE CHAPELLE	Captain Bryske 2/Siege Battery reported unable to confirm BLUE FLAG at point 'B' – communication with O.C. in O.P. broke down.	
9.10 am. do	O.C. No 1 Group Heavy Artillery reported that 8th Division Infantry had reached NEUVE CHAPELLE Church.	
9.12 am. do	48th How: Bde R.F.A. reported 18 pr. firing short on point B – 9th Bde R.F.A. asked to rectify.	
9.15 am. do	4th Bde R.F.A. reported our Infantry at point B were being shelled by German battery – direction not known. This was communicated to O.C. No 1 Group Heavy Artillery.	
9.17 am. do	9th Brigade R.F.A. reported our Infantry through wire – about 100 prisoners were marched along RUE DES BERCEAUX	✗ appendices 115 & 116
9.20 am. do	4th Brigade R.F.A. reported blue flag at point P and 7th Battery ordered to increase range	
9.22 am. do	13th Brigade R.F.A. was ordered to lengthen the range of seven a bit owing to blue flag reported at point ✗P, and 8th Division at NEUVE CHAPELLE Church	
9.25 am. do	Further message from 4th Bde R.F.A. stated 200 prisoners being marched down LA BASSÉE Road to PONT LOGY.	
9.30 am. do	4th Bde R.F.A. reported battery firing short on point B and no movement beyond the trench near point B – also that telephonist reported 300 prisoners seen in RUE du BOIS.	

Army Form C. 2118.

WAR DIARY
or
INTELLIGENCE SUMMARY.
(Erase heading not required.)

Instructions regarding War Diaries and Intelligence Summaries are contained in F. S. Regs., Part II, and the Staff Manual respectively. Title pages will be prepared in manuscript.

Hour, Date, Place.	Summary of Events and Information.	Remarks and references to Appendices
9.36 a.m. 10th March 1915. VIEILLE CHAPELLE	9th Bde R.F.A. were informed that 4th Bde R.F.A. observer reported batteries still firing short on point B*. O.C. 1/39th Garhwalis had previously asked O.C. 9th Bde for this fire to be shortened.	
9.40 a.m. do.	13th Bde R.F.A. reported O.C. Garhwalis reports his attack held up by Germans in their main trench – front and left of original line to RUE du BOIS – laying any guns on to it.	
9.42 a.m. do.	66th Battery reported battery at CROIX BARBEE firing on our own Infantry at point B*. 8th Divisional Artillery informed.	× appendices 115 + 116
9.45 a.m. do.	14th Battery R.F.A. observing Officer reported small reinforcements of enemy in S5c*.	× appendix 123
9.50 a.m. do.	4th Bde R.F.A. reported that the 2/39th Garhwalis had reported through 7th Battery that GARHWAL Bde was on line 7.P*	
9.53 a.m. do.	14th Battery R.F.A. reported German reinforcements coming up by barricade S5c* O.C. 9th Bde R.F.A. informed.	
10 a.m. do.	66th Battery R.F.A. reported British Howitzers firing at our own Infantry at point P*. Howitzers not firing anywhere near point P* but probably enemy – battery asked to confirm through C.R.A. that GARHWAL General Staff MEERUT Divnne informed. C.R.A. that GARHWAL Brigade reported might not yet clear of enemy – but later that Howitzers would be kept firing on point K* – 2/Siege Battery and 43rd How. Bde R.F.A. were informed accordingly.	

Army Form C. 2118.

WAR DIARY
or
INTELLIGENCE SUMMARY.
(Erase heading not required.)

Instructions regarding War Diaries and Intelligence Summaries are contained in F. S. Regs., Part II, and the Staff Manual respectively. Title pages will be prepared in manuscript.

Hour, Date, Place.	Summary of Events and Information.	Remarks and references to Appendices
10.6 a.m. 10th March 1915 NEUVE CHAPELLE	O.C. 14th Battery R.F.A. reported shells no longer falling short of pour L.B. × B.C. and O- 9th Bde R.F.A.	
10.12 a.m. do	30th How. Battery reported Infantry had taken informed Hdo ordered 20th and 28th Batteries to increase their range to line ××.	
10.13 a.m. do	Information received from MEERUT Divison. Report Curtis that prisoners reported German reserve on or behind, ILLIES - O.C. No.1 Group Heavy Artillery informed.	
10.30 a.m. do	O.C. No.1 Group Heavy Artillery informed that BAREILLY Brigade had reported enemy shelling our breastworks with H.E. shell - but battery not located. F.O.O. Divison reported at 10.10 a.m. that night attack of Divison had broken cross roads M 35 c × 6.3 and were about to attack trench at M 3-a 6.0 ×	× appendices 115 + 116 × appendix 123
10.34 a.m. do	H.Q. Bde R.F.A. when GARHWAL Brigade reports his line is established on SMITH DORRIEN line & reinforcements urgently required. (SMITH DORRIEN line is N PT). All R.A. units informed.	
10.37 a.m. do	66th Battery R.F.A. reported enemy appeared to be collecting between points R N O.	
10.41 a.m. do	9th Brigade R.F.A. reported 200 prisoners passed REVOLVER House. S 3 a × 4·2.	
10.51 a.m. do	Lieut. GAGE observing Officer 7th Battery R.F.A. reported that the GARHWAL Bde were urgently in need of reinforcements on the line 7 P- line getting very thin.	

Army Form C. 2118.

WAR DIARY
or
INTELLIGENCE SUMMARY.
(Erase heading not required.)

Instructions regarding War Diaries and Intelligence Summaries are contained in F. S. Regs., Part II, and the Staff Manual respectively. Title pages will be prepared in manuscript.

Hour, Date, Place.	Summary of Events and Information.	Remarks and references to Appendices
10.55 a.m. 10th March 1915 NEUVE CHAPELLE	O.C Brigade R.F.A. reported our Infantry said to be in possession of houses at Mr 19th Battery ordered to increase range 150 yds and search forward. All R.A. units informed — Confirmed by 14th Battery R.F.A. at 11.54 a.m. — O.C N°1 Group Heavy Artillery informed accordingly at 12.13 p.m.	
11.5 a.m. do	Information received from MEERUT Division Report Centre that our men reported at 11.3 a.m. one company infantry moving W. from HERLIES — Division reported at 10.30 a.m. that ILLIES, VIOLAINES, HERLIES, AUBERS, HELPEGARBE and LORGIES all clear of troops — O.C N°1 Group Heavy Artillery informed.	× appendices 114 & 116
11.9 a.m. do	Information received from MEERUT Division Report Centre that JEHRA Dn Brigade were then going forward to support GARHWAL Brigade — all R.A. units informed —	× appendix 123
11.21 a.m. do	O.C 44th Battery R.F.A reported Lieut CAMMELL wounded. This Officer was observing fire of 44th Battery in trench at PORT ARTHUR (see report by Lieut BUCHAN at 2.45 p.m)	×
11.30 a.m. do	14th Battery R.F.A. observing officers reported our Infantry visible at point M	
11.45 a.m. do	O.C N°1 Group Heavy Artillery informed think it was suggested that PIPSQUEAK gun at S.28 & 3.4 may be culprit shelling trenches at point Bt Houses at S.17a × 5.8 worthy of attention — O.C N°1 Group replied at 12.12 p.m that PIPSQUEAK mentioned had already been hammered and thought to be quiet.	

Army Form C. 2118.

WAR DIARY
or
INTELLIGENCE SUMMARY.

(Erase heading not required.)

Instructions regarding War Diaries and Intelligence Summaries are contained in F. S. Regs., Part II, and the Staff Manual respectively. Title pages will be prepared in manuscript.

Hour, Date, Place.	Summary of Events and Information.	Remarks and references to Appendices
11.53 am 10th March 1915. YEILLE CHAPELLE	66th Battery reported that he appeared to hold points D O and P – German men road between M and N No 2 a communicating trench – Germans appeared to be passing between N and O to attack B.	× Appendices 115 + 116
12.20 p.m. do	OC 9th Bde R.F.A. ordered 20th and 28th Batteries to render all help to the GARHWAL attack.	
12.25 p.m. do	Meerut Duroan verbally asked for points K A L shelled – 2nd Seige and 43rd How.Bde Brigade ordered to carry this out.	
12.28 p.m. do	OC No1 Group Heavy Artillery informed that aeroplane report at 10.40 am stated guns at BOIS du BIEZ S 12×a 1.8 and S 6 C 5.5 – this information has received from the MEERUT Duroan Report Centre. cancelled order to shell point L – message of 12.25 p.m. 2nd Seige and 43rd Brigade R.F.A. corrected accordingly.	× Appendix 123
12.30 p.m. do	OC No1 Group Heavy Artillery stated that an report received which said Column of Infantry – about a battalion – seen moving towards BOIS du BIEZ along road T 7 d 4. Head of Column also here at 11.45.a.m × × O.P.T. Art 9th Brigade R.F.A reported GARHWAL Brigade holding line C and B –	
12.40 p.m. do	MEERUT Duroan Report Centre 3 companies held up by M.G. would attack on point C from direction D – stated that DEHRA DUN Bde. units were informed and ordered to exercise care PORT ARTHUR – all R.A. units were informed and ordered to exercise care to lift fire in good time	
1.4. p.m.	66th Battery shelled by a 4" Howitzer – no damage done.	
1.30. 6.4. p.m. do	in accordance with verbal order from General Staff MEERUT Duroan at 43rd Brigade ordered, if possible, to cover fire accurately S. of letter C which we to shell into net work of trenches immediately S. of letter C which we were then attacking – also to turn battery on to trenches at letter L.	
1.31. p.m. do		

Army Form C. 2118.

WAR DIARY
or
INTELLIGENCE SUMMARY.
(Erase heading not required.)

Instructions regarding War Diaries and Intelligence Summaries are contained in F. S. Regs., Part II, and the Staff Manual respectively. Title pages will be prepared in manuscript.

Hour, Date, Place.	Summary of Events and Information.	Remarks and references to Appendices
1.45 p.m. 10th March 1915. VEILLE CHAPELLE	GARHWAL Brigade reported German gun in position at edge of BOIS du BIEZ close to third farm house S.W. from X was causing casualties to 1/39th Gurkhas. Lt. No 1 Group was asked to turn heavy battery on and knock it out. 13th Brigade R.F.A. also shelled this position in conjunction with the heavies. Observing officer of 114th Battery R.F.A. in PORT ARTHUR reported enemy still held portion of fire trench in S.4.d.8.7. about 100 yds.	× Appendices 115 & 116
2. p.m. do.	Lt. 13th Brigade R.F.A. finding the expenditure of ammunition to be something like 190 rounds per gun – gave orders to batteries to slow down their rate of fire unless a higher rate was evidently required – Slow rate of fire was ordered to all batteries at 3. p.m.	× Appendix 123
2.12 p.m. do.	20th Battery R.F.A. reported that ½ Battalion London Territorials were forming in PORT ARTHUR to assault C× and that it was believed Seaforths were to make a flank attack from our left in support.	
2.16 p.m. do.	28th Battery R.F.A. reported they had stopped firing as infantry complained that a captured trench near B× group was being shelled and the 20th Battery trench officer saw no movement in that area.	
2.27 p.m. do.	A forward observation officer reported our infantry holding M – 57th How. Battery was asked to stop firing at L.×	
2.30.p.m. do.	14th Battery R.F.A. reported AUBERS Church on fire at 1.49 p.m.	
2.34 p.m. do.	It was reported from Observation Post at PORT ARTHUR that Howitzer Battery hit house S.4.d.7.7. at 2.8.p.m. – 43rd How. Brigade was asked that battery firing should endeavour to hit trench 50 yards to south where enemy were.	

WAR DIARY or INTELLIGENCE SUMMARY

Army Form C. 2118.

Hour, Date, Place.	Summary of Events and Information.	Remarks and references to Appendices
2.35 p.m. 10th March 1915 VIEILLE CHAPELLE	Lieut D.A. BUCHAN, 2nd Battery R.F.A. reported to Lt. Col. Btt Bde R.F.A. as follows:- "Original advance of Garhwalis checked after first motion. No British officers of the regiment were present at Lieut G.H. CAMMELL, 114th Battery R.F.A. endeavoured to lead the men in the trench on after the others - He was hit and fell about 15 yds beyond our parapet - only four men followed him who were all hit - No. 1131 Private V. THOMPSON, the Black Watch, went out and brought Lieut CAMMELL in, being himself wounded in doing so."	
2.54 p.m. do	20th Battery Forward Officer reported attack on C now waiting for Seaforths and that some H.E. shell appears to be bursting over C.	× appendices 115 & 116
2.56 p.m. do	19th Battery reported that G.O.C. GARHWAL Brigade said attack on C had been stopped as some battery was shelling it and hitting our own men and that he wished fire to be stopped.	× appendix 123
3 p.m. do	Information received from Major Gourre H.F. MERCER, C.B. A.D.C. R.A. through Lt. No. 1 Group Heavy Artillery that 4th Corps commenced further advance on AUBERS Ridge at 2 p.m.	
3.15 p.m. do	GARHWAL Brigade asked for guns now shelling about C to turn on to houses E. of LA BASSEE Road in S.5.C. as Infantry could not advance - 43rd How. Brigade were asked to comply.	
3.27 p.m. do	9th Brigade R.F.A. reported Seaforths attacking point C.	
3.45 p.m. do	PIPSQUEAK shelled 114th Battery's Observation Post - 6 rounds were fired at DISTILLERY S.17.c. and PIPSQUEAK stopped.	
3.50 p.m. do	9th Brigade R.F.A. reported that point C apparently held by only about 50 Germans - This Report held up operations of our whole attack - and suggested probably a counter attack would be launched from this direction.	

Army Form C. 2118.

WAR DIARY
or
INTELLIGENCE SUMMARY.
(Erase heading not required.)

Instructions regarding War Diaries and Intelligence Summaries are contained in F. S. Regs., Part II, and the Staff Manual respectively. Title pages will be prepared in manuscript.

Hour, Date, Place.	Summary of Events and Information.	Remarks and references to Appendices
3.50 p.m. 10th March 1915. VIEILLE CHAPELLE	9th Brigade R.F.A. reported DEHRA DUN Brigade followed by JULLUNDUR Brigade were about to move on road running along Wedge of BOIS du BIEZ. 19th Battery R.F.A. reported GARHWAL Brigade wanted screen of artillery fire from point A* though point K to the houses 300 yards S.E of M* to cover the straightening out of the line round C*. 19th Battery ordered to creep from houses to roadway to West – the 20th and 28th Batteries to divide the front from K* to round to End and sweep with shell fire on their respective points – G.O.C. No 1 Group Heavy Artillery was asked to help with heavies see 4.1. p.m.	×Appendices 115 & 116
3.52 p.m. do	At No 1 Group Heavy Artillery was informed that mounted German Officer reported hostile batteries located – one at S6a* 6-true at S11b* (central) and one near cross roads S17a* – this information was received from MEERUT Division Report Centre.	×Appendix 123
3.58 p.m. do	At No 1 Group Heavy Artillery informed that report from Aeronautics III 1st Army report battery flashes at A6a O.6.	
4.1. p.m. do	At No 1 Group Heavy Artillery informed that MEERUT Division about to launch attack on BOIS du BIEZ and suggested he should order heavies to shell BOIS du BIEZ lightly but intensify fire as advance progressed.	
4.36 p.m. do	O.C's 14th, 9th and 13th Bdes R.F.A. were informed that MEERUT Division about to attack on line of road running S.W along Western edge of BOIS du BIEZ and on through BOIS du BIEZ – their objective being the Eastern edge of BOIS du BIEZ – and ordered to help scene of fire ahead of our attack.	
4.45 p.m. do	MEERUT Division Report Centre stated that prisoners reported hostile battery at T7d* 4 – 14th Battery opened fire on ground within round 55ft to on BOIS du BIEZ	

Army Form C. 2118.

WAR DIARY
or
INTELLIGENCE SUMMARY.
(Erase heading not required.)

Instructions regarding War Diaries and Intelligence Summaries are contained in F. S. Regs., Part II, and the Staff Manual respectively. Title pages will be prepared in manuscript.

Hour, Date, Place.	Summary of Events and Information.	Remarks and references to Appendices
4.51.p.m. 10th March 1915. NEUVE CHAPELLE.	8th Divisional Artillery wired that 6" shells reported falling in our trenches about M 35 – d*2.8 believed to be our own – O. No 1 Group. Heavy Artillery informed.	
5.p.m. do	2/Siege Battery reported that the Seaforths and Gurkhas attacked along the trench in S 4 d*8.14 up to the fire trench taken earlier in the day by the Garhwalis – there they found a large number of Germans who surrendered – they then moved in two ands [twos and] point M*. Just before their attack we saw about 150 or 200 Germans retiring along the communication trench for – into – point B*. There they opened an excellent target for Chupril but no battery seemed to be then engaged. 2/Siege commenced shelling cross roads in S 5 T*9.1 but had to stop as observers not possible in the dark. The Germans that fell back on point M* appeared to have thrown away their equipment and some their rifles (but this is not certain) they were in a great hurry.	× Appendices 115 & 116

× Appendix 123 |
5.15. p.m. do	Information received from the D* – NEUVE CHAPELLE on the BOIS DU BIEZ at 4.26 p.m.	
5.20. p.m. do	20th Battery R.F.A. reported C* had been taken –	
5.30. p.m. do	61st Battery R.F.A. co-operated with attack of MEERUT Division by firing Fire drawn through BOIS DU BIEZ –	
6.8. p.m. do	2/Siege Battery shelled Germans retreating in direction of M* but not to spend [damaged?] the position. Orders were issued to 43rd Hvy Bde
6.20. p.m. do	2/ Siege Battery to keep out anything on point L. 14th Battery R.J.A. reported GARHWAL Brigade supports were going up from direction of Crescent Trench. ×	O.F.A. the night two – 1 battery out A.F.A. the night south of K. Submit new R* 1 battery Sth H. A. 1 battery road junction in S*. H.d.
6.27. p.m. do	O.C. 40th Battery reported point C taken by Seaforths at 5.30.p.m.	
6.37. p.m. do	O.C. 43rd Howitzer Brigade R.F.A. ordered to maintain very slow and irregular rate of fire on night line ordered	

WAR DIARY
or
INTELLIGENCE SUMMARY.
(Erase heading not required.)

Army Form C. 2118.

Hour, Date, Place.	Summary of Events and Information.	Remarks and references to Appendices
7.4.p.m. 10th March 1915. VIEILLE CHAPELLE	The batteries of the Hvy, 9th and 13th Brigades R.F.A. were ordered to maintain a very slow rate of fire on the eastern edge of BOIS du BIEZ –	
7.33 p.m. do	Hvy Bde R.F.A. ordered to have night lines laid out on eastern edge of BOIS du BIEZ and to fire a few occasional rounds at irregular intervals	
7.48 p.m. do	13th Bde R.F.A. ordered to have night lines laid out on N.E. corner of BOIS du BIEZ — and not to fire unless ordered. 9th Bde R.F.A. ordered to have night lines laid out on LIGNY Le PETIT and to fire occasional irregular bursts on this line to East of BOIS du BIEZ	
8.30.p.m. do	At 8.30 p.m. orders were issued to all batteries to discontinue irregular bursts unless occasion should arise for opening fire.	
8.55 p.m. do	8th Battery reported German field battery firing from about S.17 z (probably S.10.a.9.5) and observation Post and trenches near S.10.a.9.5. With reference to the Operation of the day a officer of the 9th Bde R.F.A. reported that Chevaux de frise type of barbed wire was in front of ordinary low wire entanglement — the wires about 6 yards depth – the former was crumpled up and the latter virtually ceased to exist by our fire – the Infantry were able to walk through as if no obstacle had existed. — O.C. 13th Bde R.F.A. confirmed this. Early in the afternoon RICHEBOURG was shelly. several H.E. were dropped into the town near the 2nd large Battery's offices Minca M 32.c – only 50% of these exploded. The hostile aircraft was seen today – between 6.45 a.m. and 5.20 p.m. 8 British and 5 French machines were seen. Sketch Maps 5000 illustrating Phase I of operations is attached ditto Map 5000 illustrating Phases II and III of operations is attached	✱ appendix 111 ☩ appendix 114 ✕ appendix 123 ✚ appendix 1135 ✱ appendix 116

Army Form C. 2118.

WAR DIARY
or
INTELLIGENCE SUMMARY.
(Erase heading not required.)

Instructions regarding War Diaries and Intelligence Summaries are contained in F.S. Regs., Part II. and the Staff Manual respectively. Title pages will be prepared in manuscript.

Hour, Date, Place	Summary of Events and Information	Remarks and references to Appendices
12.40. a.m. 11th March 1915 NEUVE CHAPELLE	BAREILLY Brigade reported enemy probing in between ORCHARD Redoubt and CRESCENT trench and asked for guns to be turned on to enemy's trenches at this point. LAHORE Divisional Artillery asked to turn guns on to point indicated and 43rd Howitzer Brigade was ordered to open slow rate of fire on points A and K as soon as possible - 4th, 9th and 13th Brigades R.F.A. also informed and ordered to inform any Artillery Brigades of LAHORE Division near their own Headquarters -	
1.55.a.m. do	9th Bde. R.I.A. informed the 40th Howitzer Battery -	
4.a.m. do	O.C. 13th Brigade R.F.A. reported that enemy pushing on between ORCHARD Redoubt and CRESCENT Redoubt. O.C. 13th Bde. R.F.A. informed the 5th and 18th Brigades R.F.A. (LAHORE Divisional Artillery).	
	Operation Order No.11 by C.R.A. MEERUT Division issued by motor cyclist	✱ Appendix 117
6.45 am do	7th Battery R.F.A. directed fire on area M.11 - S.6.d.9.9 to S.6.a.1.3	✱
6.59 a.m. do	20th Battery R.F.A. reported Germans searching area S.3.b. with shrapnel	✱ Appendices 115 + 116
7 am to 8 am do	11th Heavy Battery neutralised enemy batteries at S.17 which were inclined to give trouble.	✱
7.50 am do	Report from BAREILLY Brigade, timed 7.35 a.m. received through MEERUT Divisional Report Centre stated that enemy were shelling our Eastern front from a Southern direction at 7.a.m. - O.C. No.1 Group Heavy Artillery was informed. fire to be maintained on A and K and G.O.C. Division asked that wire cables for this were sent to 43rd Howitzer Brigade and 2nd Siege Battery.	✱ Appendix 123
8 a.m. do	20th Battery R.F.A. reported through 9th Brigade that point M was occupied by scouts of Garhwalis.	

(3 29 G) W 4141-433 100,000 9/14 H W V Forms/C. 2118/10

Army Form C. 2118.

WAR DIARY
or
INTELLIGENCE SUMMARY.
(Erase heading not required.)

Instructions regarding War Diaries and Intelligence Summaries are contained in F.S. Regs, Part II. and the Staff Manual respectively. Title pages will be prepared in manuscript.

Hour, Date, Place	Summary of Events and Information	Remarks and references to Appendices
8.24 a.m. 11th March 1915. NEUVE CHAPELLE	Information received from MEERUT Division report centre that attack held up by machine gun fire on both flanks – not located enemy & thick fog. Front of attack still on River LAYES – 4th, 9th and 13th Brigades were ordered to turn heavy bursts of fire on Western edge of BOIS du BIEZ – point M which Heavy Artillery were also asked to search our field guns.	
8.30 a.m. do	O.C. 4th Brigade R.F.A. reported German Heavy Battery firing on LA COUTURE from direction of LORGIES. O.C. No 1 Group Heavy Artillery asked to engage.	
8.41 a.m. do	O.C. 9th Brigade R.F.A. ordered whole of his Brigade Ammunition Column to R x 35. O.C. Ammunition Column ordered to inform Infantry Brigade.	x Appendices 115 & 116
8.45 a.m. do	66th Battery R.F.A. fired series of bursts of fire on enemy's machine guns on N.W. edge of BOIS du BIEZ	x Appendix 123
8.50 a.m. do	MEERUT Division ordered shell fire on point A and trenches W. of LA BASSÉE Road between A* and R* and trenches W. of LA BASSÉE reported in N* and R* and between these two points – 6 enemy machine guns supposed to be in and near A* – also from A to S.10 central. Garhwalis LAHORE Divisional Artillery asked (verbally) to comply – 43rd Hoy Brigade was asked to deal sternly with A* 7th Battery R.F.A. fired on enemy's machine guns in area S.5.d. 9.9.6. S.6.a* 1.3.	
8.55 a.m. do	Enemy shelled 20th and 26th Batteries R.F.A. with 6" gun – not located – 3 shell nearby hit Headquarters billet of 9th Brigade R.F.A. at about same time.	
9.5 a.m. do	General Staff MEERUT Division asked for fire on K x to stop up fire continued on A* and Redoubt behind it. 114th Heavy Battery shelled W. end of BOIS du BIEZ.	
9.7 a.m. do	2/Siege Battery ordered to stop firing on K for the present.	
9.10 a.m. do	MEERUT Division asked for shell fire on M and group of houses East of M. LAHORE Divisional Artillery asked to comply with a battery	

Army Form C. 2118.

WAR DIARY
or
INTELLIGENCE SUMMARY.
(Erase heading not required.)

Instructions regarding War Diaries and Intelligence Summaries are contained in F.S. Regs., Part II. and the Staff Manual respectively. Title pages will be prepared in manuscript.

Hour, Date, Place	Summary of Events and Information	Remarks and references to Appendices
9.15 am 11th March 1915. NEUVE CHAPELLE	At 4th Brigade R.J.A reported that Observing Officer with DEHRA DUN Brigade states large masses of enemy crowding into trenches near M.× 14th Battery ordered to take them on. 4th, 9th and 13th Brig. also R.J.A. were ordered to let them have it hot and sharp for a bit - jerk out for bursts and then steady again.	
9.30 am — do —	14th Battery R.J.A fired a few rounds gun fire behind S11a 6.8 as enemy were reported there.	
9.35 am — do —	Observing Officer 13th Brigade R.J.A. reported that our Infantry were firing through L NEUVE CHAPELLE towards BOIS du BIEZ	
9.40 am — do —	8th Battery opened rapid fire for about 10 minutes on Germans' moustache in front of our line. Enemy shelled RICHEBOURG with "WILLIES" shells also dropping about 200 yds East of VILLE of Headquarters 9th Bde R.J.A.	× appendices 115 & 116
9.55 am — do —	14th Battery R.J.A opened slow fire in front of BOIS du BIEZ with sharp bursts 7th Battery R.J.A. fired on Germans massed on N.W corner of BOIS du BIEZ also a few rounds at same area at 10.20 a.m.	
10.21 am — do —	4th Brigade R.J.A reported that Observing officer with DEHRA DUN Brigade states large group of Germans in BOIS du BIEZ and asks for fire on road M.J.— 8th Bde ordered sharp bursts of fire to be turned on	— ?
10.25 am — do —	8th Battery fired for two minutes on N.W corner of BOIS du BIEZ	
10.32 am — do —	At 8th Brigade R.J.A reported Nr Shelley LACOUTURE pretty freely — Ot. No 1 Group Heavy Artillery asked to deal with it	
10.37 am — do —	At 14th Battery R.J.A reported no movement could be seen - observing Officer with DEHRA DUN Bde reported very heavy bombardment of NEUVE CHAPELLE and trenches to South - Intention for shoot appearing the same at No 1 Group Heavy Artillery informed accordingly.	

Army Form C. 2118.

WAR DIARY
or
INTELLIGENCE SUMMARY.
(Erase heading not required.)

Instructions regarding War Diaries and Intelligence Summaries are contained in F. S. Regs., Part II. and the Staff Manual respectively. Title pages will be prepared in manuscript.

Hour, Date, Place	Summary of Events and Information	Remarks and references to Appendices
10.45 a.m. 11th March 1915. NEUVE CHAPELLE.	Information received that German counter-attack advancing from North corner of BOIS du BIEZ on NEUVE CHAPELLE. O.C. No 1 Group Heavy Artillery asked 6" gun on to N.W. corner of wood at once – 4th, 9th and 13th Brigades R.F.A. were ordered to intensify fire in that direction.	
11.10 a.m. do	6th Battery R.F.A. increased rate of fire on German counter attack towards NEUVE CHAPELLE.	
11.15 a.m. do	7th Battery R.F.A. fired on German counter attack from North end of BOIS du BIEZ – Observing officer reported fire very effective.	
11.25 a.m. do	66th Battery R.F.A. reported 18 pr battery shelling our own Infantry at point N – 9th and 13th Brigades R.F.A. were informed.	
11.40 a.m. do	Advanced Observing Officer 13th Brigade R.F.A. with Infantry reported two hostile guns in action 100 yds N.E. of BOIS du BIEZ – O.C. No 1 Group Heavy Artillery asked to knock them out – 8th Dehra Dun Artillery also informed.	appendices 115 + 116
12.15 p.m. do	7th Battery R.F.A. fired on section of guns S.W. of 56 a 7.8 which observing officer located.	× appendix 123
12.20 p.m. do	Observing officer 4th Brigade R.F.A. with DEHRA DUN Brigade reported our Infantry soon to advance – O.C. No 1 Group Heavy Artillery informed and referred to Wyndle on point U – 13th Brigade R.F.A. informed re slow fire on road M×U× and 43rd Howitzer Brigade to warm 40th How: Battery.	
12.28 p.m. do	9th Brigade R.F.A. reported enemy 4 gun howitzer Battery – probable line LORGIES – shelling S 3 c 2 – O.C. No 1 Group Heavy Artillery also informed.	
12.50 p.m. do	All Brigades R.F.A. informed that 4th Corps ordered advance to commence shortly and that over 25th Infantry Brigade would advance alongside our DEHRA DUN Brigade when trench established.	

Forms/C.2118/10
(9296) W 14141—453 100,000 9/14 H W V

Army Form C. 2118.

WAR DIARY
or
INTELLIGENCE SUMMARY.
(Erase heading not required.)

Instructions regarding War Diaries and Intelligence Summaries are contained in F.S. Regs., Part II. and the Staff Manual respectively. Title pages will be prepared in manuscript.

Hour, Date, Place	Summary of Events and Information	Remarks and references to Appendices
1.12.p.m. 11th March 1915. VEUILLE CHAPELLE	All Brigades R.F.A. were ordered to be prepared to open very heavy fire for 4 minutes on tasks allotted along western edge of BOIS du BIEZ at very short notice – Code word "Open" – All were warned to avoid point M occupied by us – after 4 minutes intense fire to proceed with phase 2. This was in connection with infantry assault.	× Appendix 115+16
2.p.m. do	30th How. Battery reported 2 hits on machine guns – Enemy dropped a large number of "Black Marias" in front of 66th Battery.	
2.7.p.m. do	20th Battery R.F.A. reported that O.C. Leicesters stated large body of enemy lying on ground along what appeared to be headcover from S11 7.0.7. to S11 7.9.7. – O.C. Leicesters believed counter attack going to be attempted – 20th Battery was ordered to keep careful look out in direction of S11 7.	+Appendix /23
2.8 to 2.12.pm do	Batteries of 4th, 9th, 13th and 43rd (How) Brigades R.F.A. opened very heavy fire on tasks allotted along western edge of BOIS du BIEZ preparatory to infantry assault.	
2.30.p.m. do	14th Battery R.F.A. reported PORT ARTHUR shelled by enemy howitzer	
2.50.p.m. do	9th Brigade R.F.A. reported enemy 4 gun howitzer battery bearing line S4C – M33a with shrapnel. O.C. No.1 Group Heavy Artillery informed.	
3.p.m. do	9th Brigade R.F.A. reported enemy howitzer battery – probably LORGIES – shelling N. side S37 & 8.4 along which our troops now moving up. O.C. No.1 Group Heavy Artillery was informed accordingly. 14th Battery reported our infantry seemed to be attacking northern edge of BOIS du BIEZ which was apparently successful.	

WAR DIARY or INTELLIGENCE SUMMARY

Army Form C. 2118.

Hour, Date, Place	Summary of Events and Information	Remarks and references to Appendices
3.30.p.m. 11th March 1915. VIEILLE CHAPELLE	OC 9th Brigade R.F.A. reported that enemy still in BOIS du BIEZ, Garhwalis and Leicesters not advanced —	
4.20.p.m. do	14th Battery R.F.A. reported RICHEBOURG and surroundings shelled by enemy including heavy howitzers. 44th Battery was shelled a little — no casualties.	
4.30.p.m. do	9th Brigade R.F.A. reported enemy's howitzers (LORGIES?) shelling trenches around PORT ARTHUR — OC No. 1 Group Heavy Artillery informed. Enemy "8" shells near Headquarters Divisional Artillery Meerut Division	⊕ French gun with special fuze. —
4.38.p.m. do	OC No. 1 Group Heavy Artillery informed. OC 44th Brigade R.F.A. reported heavy shell from direction of RUE duc MARAIS (S 28 b 9/10?) dropped into LA COUTURE all day — at No. 1 Group Heavy Artillery informed accordingly.	× appendices 115 +116
4.40.p.m. do	114th Battery R.F.A. reported PORT ARTHUR being shelled with H.E. at 4.30.p.m.	× appendix 123
4.50.p.m. do	Orders issued to OC 43rd Brigade (How.) R.F.A. for night lines — one battery on Rebentif. Also trenches to South and 100 yards to East of it. — Two batteries due N of houses and road from M× to J× inclusive — between K× and M×	
4.55.p.m. do	2/Howe Battery ordered to lay night lines on trenches between K× and M× and Southward from line R M. —	
5.p.m. do	Orders issued to 9th Brigade R.F.A. to arrange night lines to cover from M× to S×, U×, 5.5× both inclusive — so believed withdrawing to line T× P× O× C× B× tonight owing to "Black Marias" in front of 66k Enemy dropped large number of "Black Marias" in front of 66k Battery, slight damage to two gun emplacements — Battery Commander and Captain also covered with mud, otherwise no damage.	
5.55.p.m. do	Night lines from S× S× Q× S× to 5th Bde 2.3 both inclusive — OC 1/Brigade informed in case of 9th Bde R.F.A.	

WAR DIARY
or
INTELLIGENCE SUMMARY.
(Erase heading not required.)

Army Form C. 2118.

Hour, Date, Place	Summary of Events and Information	Remarks and references to Appendices
5.10. p.m. 11th March 1915. NEUVE CHAPELLE	CL 13th Brigade R.F.A. ordered to bring up eight horse to cover line of front and houses from S6 x 2.3 to S6 x 5.9 both inclusive - OL Brigade informed we withdrawal as were OL 1 L.K. + 9th Brigade R.F.A.	+appendix 123
5.22. p.m. do	9th Brigade R.F.A. reported that at 4.33 p.m. it had been reported that Infantry attack had reached BOIS du BIEZ.	
5.35. p.m. do	9th Brigade R.F.A. reported that a further a later report stated Garhwalis and Seaforths had not yet moved - these units were right and left arks of Brie and German rifle fire still coming from BOIS - this information from point D at 5. P.M.	+appendices 115+116
7.45 p.m. do	BAREILLY Brigade reported that R.A. Observation Officer for RITZ Saw Germans collecting at 6.40 p.m. about figure 10 of square S.10 and asked for batteries to be warned - BAREILLY Bde was informed that necessary dispositions had been made. Nature of huge events attacked Several enemys new guns including 8.2 howitzers appeared which had not been seen before - unable to locate any flashes but from the general direction and hinge-up taken on the craters it was estimated that their position was near AUBERS. 5" 9" and other shell fell in neighbourhood of Headquarters billet of 13th Brigade R.F.A, at frequent intervals from 9 a.m. to 4 p.m. probably trying for 4.7" or 9.2" near LA COUTURE - no casualties. NEUVE CHAPELLE was shelled continuously during the day and our Heavy Wood Shell - one howitzer shell from direction of LA BASSEE. original from French running NW from PORT ARTHUR received a lot of shrapnel shell fire throughout the day.	+appendix 118 

Army Form C. 2118.

WAR DIARY
or
INTELLIGENCE SUMMARY.
(Erase heading not required.)

Instructions regarding War Diaries and Intelligence Summaries are contained in F.S. Regs., Part II. and the Staff Manual respectively. Title pages will be prepared in manuscript.

Hour, Date, Place	Summary of Events and Information	Remarks and references to Appendices
12th March 1915 VIEILLE CHAPELLE.	Day opened very thick mist: observation very difficult	
5.15. am — do —	Communication between 9th Brigade R.F.A. Headquarters and the batteries of the brigade cut by enemy's shell fire which was directed on RICHEBOURG. Morning very thick and misty - observation very difficult.	
6.a.m — do —	2nd Siege Battery fired a few rounds on point K and round right of point M.	
6.8 am — do —	2nd Battery R.F.A. reported that Infantry started heavy attack on PORT ARTHUR - LAHORE Divisional Artillery informed. O.C. 44th Brigade R.F.A. has asked to inform 18th Bde R.F.A. - 40th How. Battery was asked to assist by fire to S.E. of bombtitle with one coy enemy - 9th Brigade R.F.A. was also informed -	× Appendices 115&116
6.15.am — do —	28th Battery opened fire on point M at request of Infantry.	
6.30 am — do —	9th Brigade R.F.A. reported he had ordered batteries to assist, & bombtitle, against attack on PORT ARTHUR with due economy.	
6.33 am — do —	O.C. No 1 Group Heavy Artillery informed that enemy was making heavy attack on PORT ARTHUR from 6.a.m. and asking for heavy batteries to assist on LORGIES crossroads and RUE du MARAIS and crossroads S17a	× Appendix 123
6.50 am — do —	13th Brigade R.F.A. reported enemy attack on CRESCENT Trench driven back by Black Watch - this was communicated to 4K, 9K and 43rd (How.) Brigade R.F.A.	
7.6 am — do —	43rd (How.) Brigade R.F.A. asked to open fire on A and K at once.	
7.20 am — do —	2/ Siege Battery reported Germans in communication trench 75 yards in front of CRESCENT trench surrendering & considerable number	

(3 29 6) W4141-483 100,000 9/14 H W V Forms/C. 2118/10

Army Form C. 2118.

WAR DIARY
or
INTELLIGENCE SUMMARY.
(Erase heading not required.)

Instructions regarding War Diaries and Intelligence Summaries are contained in F.S. Regs., Part II. and the Staff Manual respectively. Title pages will be prepared in manuscript.

Hour, Date, Place	Summary of Events and Information	Remarks and references to Appendices
7.30 a.m. 12th March 1915. NEUVE CHAPELLE	2/Siege Battery fired a few rounds at Redoubt S.10 & S.5.9 where a lot of Germans were known to be.	
7.45 a.m. do.	9th Brigade R.F.A. reported that DEHRA DUN Brigade stated counter attack round point A* and B* easily beaten off - action seemed more chiefly artillery - all quiet recruits of NEUVE CHAPELLE.	x Appendices 115 & 116
7.55 a.m. do.	20th and 26th Batteries R.F.A. shelled by enemy 6" Howitzer and field guns.	
8. a.m. do.	66th Battery R.F.A. reported we had captured new trench and that prisoners could be plainly seen at 7.05 a.m. - the trench was thought to be one reported as dug during night within 30 yards of our.	
8.7 a.m. do.	66th Battery R.F.A. reported German Battery fog direction of LORGIES shelter S.10 K - new trench reported in S.10 K - 114th Battery report PORT ARTHUR heavily shelled from S.17 a - honors to that area were shelled by 114th Battery R.J.A. The above reports were communicated to O.C. N°.1 Group Heavy Artillery.	x Appendix 123 x Appendix 119
8.15 a.m. do.	Operation Order N°.12 by C.R.A. MEERUT Division issued by mounted orderly.	
8.45 a.m. do.	2nd Siege Battery reported that wounded officer from NEUVE CHAPELLE states that it that of his relief the attack there was repulsed.	
9.2 a.m. do.	4th Bde R.F.A. reported - 14th Battery reconnoitred advanced position this morning - enemy shelling positions with gun and howitzer fire - some casualties amongst men billeted there. That slowly stream of wounded and prisoners came up LA BASSEE road. Men of Notts and Derbys said they were driven out of trench but could attack had rejoined line capturing many prisoners - Northamptons said to have been driven out of trench further North and gained in places ground that no ground had been lost.	

WAR DIARY
or
INTELLIGENCE SUMMARY.
(Erase heading not required.)

Army Form C. 2118.

Hour, Date, Place	Summary of Events and Information	Remarks and references to Appendices
9.12. a.m. 12th March 1915. NEUVE CHAPELLE	9th Brigade R.F.A. reported enemy's big inch howitzer shelling area S.33-7.6 to M.33 a 1.8 very heavily - this was communicated to O.C. N°1 Group Heavy Artillery.	
9.13 a.m. do	Report from Observation Officer with SIRHIND Brigade that 9.6.a.m. Stated heavy bombardment and fire attack - Germans occupied trench abandoned last night by Gurkhas between S.5-3-3.1 and S.5-3-3.5 - Coal boxes bombards NEUVE CHAPELLE. O.C. N°1 Group Heavy Artillery informed.	
9.37 a.m. do	9th Brigade R.F.A. reported 28th Battery Kinch Officer sent into battery by O.C. Seaforths for Artillery support - all communication broken. Houses S.5 c 41 heavily strongly held by enemy - this observed from C. 2nd Siege & 43rd How. Bde asked if could engage opportunity.	× appendices 115 & 116
9.43 a.m. do	2nd Siege Battery reported Gurkhas bombing above Germans that had trench near S.10 & 8.7 which appear to be unoccupied.	
9.50. a.m. do	MEERUT Division reports received that operations postponed for 2 hours and consequently Infantry assault on BOIS du BIEZ would take place at 1.P.M. instead of 11.A.M - All units informed by telephone. 2nd Battery Kinch officer reported houses at S.5 c 4.1 strong by him by enemy - day cold to be observed from trenches (C×).	× appendix 123
10.40 a.m. do	2nd Battery R.F.A. opened fire on S.11 a 5.3 at request of G.O.C. BAREILLY Bde to assist in repelling a counter attack.	
10.45 a.m. do	6.H.E. shell from enemy's guns burst near 9th Brigade R.F.A. Headquarters - Killed 8 horses and 5 mules of the 4th Black Watch & adjacent orchard.	
10.47 a.m. do	19th Battery R.F.A. reported through 13th Brigade that right of SIRHIND Bng are during attack will advance along road running through squares S.5.C × S.11.2 × S.11.C - to night & then to this flank will need strong artillery support - this was communicated to 9th Bde R.F.A., 43rd How Bde R.F.A., 2nd Siege Battery

Army Form C. 2118.

WAR DIARY
or
INTELLIGENCE SUMMARY.
(Erase heading not required.)

Instructions regarding War Diaries and Intelligence Summaries are contained in F.S. Regs., Part II. and the Staff Manual respectively. Title pages will be prepared in manuscript.

Hour, Date, Place	Summary of Events and Information	Remarks and references to Appendices
11.7. a.m. 12th March 1915 NEUVE CHAPELLE	Who were asked to take great care with Phase 2 in Operation Order No.12. Col. No.1 Group Henry Battery also informs. General Staff MEERUT Divn.nal telephoned that enemy appearance of M. at 200 yds S.E. of the C. B. on N.W. front of about 300 yds out asking if artillery could help. 2nd Siege were warned out of the Bde R.F.A. ready to shoot.	
11.20. a.m. do	Forward Officer of 13th Brigade R.F.A. reported GARHWAL and BAREILLY Brigades will continue to hold present position – GARHWAL Brigade sending a garrison working party to secure houses at road junction S.11.a. & after capture by SIRHIND Brigade.	
11.23 a.m. do	2/Siege Battery reported German communication trenches at S.10 & 8.7.– field artillery are shelling them.	
12.10 p.m. do	6th Battery R.F.A. fired on Germans holding trenches from point B. to ESTAIRES – LA BASSÉE road.	× Appendices 115 & 116
12.15 p.m. do	Situation to the North was as follows – Our Infantry had captured road 500 yds N.W. of PIETRE – Bombardment proceeds on the bridge junction 250 yds N.W. of LA RUSSIE. Assault over the river LAYES and buildings at 12.30.p.m on the bridge of 25th Infantry Bde now ready to be launched.	× Appendix 123
12.30. p.m. do	7th Division announced road runner N.W. from MOULIN de PIETRE – Another 150 prisoners came in from German lines.	
1.30 p.m. do	Captain Murray Black Watch reported enemy new in force at 11. a.m. between the CRESCENT and PORT ARTHUR. 14th Battery opened slow searching fire on W corner of BOIS du BIEZ. 2nd Siege Battery bombarded point M × with good effect.	
1.35 p.m. do	114th Heavy Battery engaged battery at S.17.d with one section and neutralized it. Observing Officer of 14th Battery R.F.A. reported attack not yet launched. 14th Battery shelled Eastern edge of BOIS du BIEZ S.12.a 4.4.	

Forms/C. 2118/10

Army Form C. 2118.

WAR DIARY
or
INTELLIGENCE SUMMARY.
(Erase heading not required.)

Instructions regarding War Diaries and Intelligence Summaries are contained in F.S. Regs., Part II. and the Staff Manual respectively. Title pages will be prepared in manuscript.

Hour, Date, Place	Summary of Events and Information	Remarks and references to Appendices
1.40 p.m. 12th March 1915 VEILLE CHAPELLE	Three battalions of enemy reported in BOIS du BIEZ and more to East of it. 4th, 9th and 13th Brigades ordered to continue Search as it and also for a certain extent to East of it. 43rd Hou: Brigade were ordered to turn one section by battery for searching fire on Eastern half of wood. Right flank being watched all the through - 2/Siege Battery also informed that Garhwalis reported their flank threatened by large number of enemy near B* and to with-draw and if possible with safety to march to do so - but not to neglect original tasks.	
1.50 p.m. do	14th Battery R.F.A. reported 25th Infantry Brigade holding first line trenches alright but are held up by enemy artillery - German Infantry returning. Our guns doing good work - Assault of TULLUNDUR Brigade begun on our right - O.C. No 1 Group Heavy Artillery informed	x Appendices 115 + 116
1.52 p.m. do	9th Brigade R.F.A. asked re assault Garhwalis now to be apparently went forward as ordered but harassed by enemy in force near B*. 43rd Hou Brigade also asked to assist.	
2 p.m. do	14th Battery R.F.A. observed slow searching fire on BOIS du BIEZ. Forward officer of 13th Brigade R.F.A. reported no change in enemy position in front of him P*+T* at 12.15. p.m.	
2.6 p.m. do	14th Battery R.F.A. fired at enemy in the trenches near LA BASSÉE road with one gun - where a party now harrying our men at B* and C*.	
2.20 p.m. do	40th Hou Battery reported Germans shelling B*. O.C. No 1 Group Heavy A.A. now informed	
2.30 p.m. do	Capt Crippo 19th Battery R.F.A. reported Howitzer Battery dropping shell short in our advanced trench in front of PORT ARTHUR - O.C. 2nd Brigade	

WAR DIARY or INTELLIGENCE SUMMARY.

Army Form C. 2118.

Hour, Date, Place	Summary of Events and Information	Remarks and references to Appendices
2.40 p.m. 12th March 1915 NEUVE CHAPELLE	4th, 9th and 13th Brigades R.F.A. were ordered to top fire on BOIS du BIEZ for present - also 43rd How. Brigade and 2nd Siege Battery who were to remain in observation of trenches allotted for Phase 1 and 2 but to seize any good opportunity - situation same.	
2.45 p.m. do	Forward officer 13th Brigade R.F.A. reports at 12.15 p.m. 1st 4th Gurkhas rushed German trench on his F.* Lately abandoned by 2/2nd Gurkhas. Over 100 prisoners captured.	×appendices 115 & 116
2.47 p.m. do	43rd How Brigade wired 40th How. Battery reported at 2.8.p.m. no signs of Infantry attacking N.W. face of BOIS du BIEZ - Germans shelling M* and road South of M.* 40th Battery shelled BOIS du BIEZ and 57K Battery firing on B*	×appendix 123
3.3. p.m. do	O.C. No.1 Group Heavy Artillery reported that battery shelling LA COUTURE at intervals for last 3 Anglo-calibre unknown but will of shell very thin. time leaving 100° from point × 5 at 5-3.	
3.5. p.m. do	Observation officer of 14th Battery R.F.A. reported general situation at 2.40 p.m. Infantry attack not yet launched. Germans in the trench from point B to barricade on LA BASSEE road having been indiscriminately shelled by both German and English crawling away in threes and fours towards the communication trenches in rear but still came even in this portion of trench.	
3.45 p.m. do	Information received from Observing Officer with SIRHIND Brigade through 4th Brigade R.F.A. that howitzer in S5 d 9.5 and portion of the triangle to the W. of that point to full of machine guns and should be heavily shelled before launching attack in that direction.	

WAR DIARY
or
INTELLIGENCE SUMMARY.
(Erase heading not required.)

Army Form C. 2118.

Instructions regarding War Diaries and Intelligence Summaries are contained in F. S. Regs., Part II. and the Staff Manual respectively. Title pages will be prepared in manuscript.

Hour, Date, Place	Summary of Events and Information	Remarks and references to Appendices
4 p.m. 12th March 1915 VEILLE CHAPELLE	O.C. 4th, 9th, 13th & 43rd (How) Brigades and 2nd Siege Battery were informed that GARHWAL Brigade stated that when they push forward they will do so via trenches to the South of point "B", as the road would require very careful watching when the work came off.	
4.4 p.m. do	Report received from point "D" through O.C. 9th Brigade R.F.A. that our troops still holding two morning line from point "P" 200 yards North of N.front of C* to B*. Gun trenches full of Infantry ready to assault but waiting for 8th Division. Hardly any rifle fire in front of our line.	× Appendices 115 & 116
4.10 p.m. do	O.C. No 1 Group informed that airman reports as follows:— "20 to 30 motor on road ILLIES to FOURNES. ILLIES seemed full of life but no formed bodies there — no movement South of the BOIS" at 3.50 p.m.	
4.19 p.m. do	Observing officer with SIRHIND Brigade reported through O.C. Brigade R.F.A. that attack held up on the line of Quin LAYES — cannot progress until attack of 8th Division gets more advanced. This was also reported by the Forward Officer of the 13th Brigade R.F.A.	
4.30 p.m. do	O.C. 9th Brigade R.F.A. reported enemy's howitzers, probably LORGIES, Shelled trenches round "PORT ARTHUR".	
4.45 p.m. do	9th Brigade R.F.A. reported that Cavalry Damier has broken through at TRIVELET (N.19.a × 5.1)	× Appendix 123
4.53 p.m. do	4th, 9th, 13th and 43rd (How) Brigades and 2nd Siege Battery were informed that there would be a repetition of the whole of the operations in connection with operation Order No 12 commencing at a time to be notified later. The only exception to be procedure is that preliminary bombardment will be for 15 minutes instead of 30 minutes. In place I will be for Heavy Artillery was also informed that LAHORE Division has got 9 to deliver an assault on exactly same line as planned for 1 p.m. today. All tasks for Artillery exactly same as for earlier.	⊕ Appendix 119

C. of N. Form/C. 2118/10   (9 29 6)   W 4141-463 100,000 9/14 H W V

WAR DIARY
or
INTELLIGENCE SUMMARY.
(Erase heading not required.)

Army Form C. 2118.

Instructions regarding War Diaries and Intelligence Summaries are contained in F.S. Regs., Part II. and the Staff Manual respectively. Title pages will be prepared in manuscript.

Hour, Date, Place	Summary of Events and Information	Remarks and references to Appendices
5.6.p.m. 12th March 1915. VIEILLE CHAPELLE.	Attack except that bombardment of both grants of an hour. Took the notified late - asked to state of advd position where task is at 12.30 p.m. Reply to Wire was "Yes".	
5.11 p.m. do	All R.A. units informed that 7th Division has taken Mill du PIETRE and M 30 a 6.10 and 600 prisoners - 8th Division still held up on own left at M 35 d. 9.4 by machine guns - enemy reported to be disorganised.	× Appendices 115 & 116
5.30 p.m. do	4th, 9th + 13th Brigades R.F.A. informed that GARHWAL Brigade asked for Artillery fire in that direction to be the range which is at present causing casualties to our line B×C×	
5.45 p.m. do	2nd. Battery R.F.A. French officer reported our Infantry still formed up ready for assault but no movement observed.	
6.30 p.m. do	All units ordered that bombardment maintain a normal rate of fire. 6.43 p.m. would commence at 5.50 p.m. and continue for 16 minutes.	× Appendix 123
6.31 p.m. do	Report received from 13th Brigade Q.F.A. that SIRHIND Brigade had reached line of river about 6 p.m. — Rifle Brigade not so far.	
6.30 p.m. do	9th and 13th Brigades were informed that no organic comn in phase 2 suggested. Sectn. fire one round, but 2 rounds keep touch with Infantry and the actual situation and act accordingly	
6.30 p.m. do	All units informed that 7th Division had captured 3 guns 7 machine guns 500 prisoners and are believed to be near AUBERS.	
7.20 p.m. do	4th, 9th and 13th Bdes ordered to stop firing in case an attack appeared not to have taken place. Arrangt. night line to form cover 400 yds. E. of edge of BOIS du BIEZ. The three Brigades on equal portions of line from S.12. C. Kh to S 6a × 10.9.	

WAR DIARY
or
INTELLIGENCE SUMMARY.
(Erase heading not required.)

Army Form C. 2118.

Hour, Date, Place	Summary of Events and Information	Remarks and references to Appendices
7.25 p.m. 12th March 1915 NEUVE CHAPELLE	66th Battery O.3.A reported Indian Corps holding line from Point S 57 through points P * O * 8th Division night to 200 yds to left near of Indian Corps – Germans hold trench 50 yds on border ―― cotes of River LAYES.	× Appendices 115 & 116
7.52 p.m. do	Right division 43rd How. Brigade – one battery on A and Redoubt to South of it – one battery on K and trenches to South of it – one battery covering our Southern front trenches.	× Appendix 123
7.50 p.m. do	Right two Siege Battery says no shot might sent with one gun actually on point M itself but not to open fire unless ordered to do so.	
9.7 p.m. do	43rd Howitzer Brigade were ordered that at 10.30 p.m. the battery that is on A and trenches to South of it to open fire on A and those trenches till 10.45 p.m. The battery on K and trenches in front of our Southern trenches to open fire on those hostile trenches from 10.30–10.45 p.m. I have ever must any fire go on Eastern side of the LA BASSEE road – the third battery had out on K not to open fire.	
9.10 p.m. do	O.C.'s 14th, 9th and 13th Brigades ordered to send within the limits of the BOIS du BIEZ on the line of their existing night line from 10.30 p.m. to 10.45 p.m. Section fire 30 seconds after fire 10.30 p.m. precisely.	
9.30 p.m. do	Orders received that Corps Commander considers mass attack tonight and will bombardment would not take place at 10.30 p.m. All R.A. units informed that operations for 10.30–10.45 p.m. cancelled.	
10.7 p.m. do	4th, 9th and 13th Brigades ordered to cancel previous orders re night lines – new night lines on Western edge of BOIS du BIEZ, each Brigade taking its pro rata U frontage allotted to them + places 1 V Howitzer Brigade was ordered to man all batteries to take exceptional

WAR DIARY
or
INTELLIGENCE SUMMARY.
(Erase heading not required.)

Army Form C. 2118.

Hour, Date, Place	Summary of Events and Information	Remarks and references to Appendices
	Care of every round of ammunition. Shells from PIPSQUEAK were falling on our Bde Battery all afternoon – most of them falling in RICHEBOURG. The enemy were shelling my community all the morning. Received from NEUVE CHAPELLE to PORT ARTHUR through S37* and S42* — S37* and S42*.	*Appendix 123
	Al. reported that Germans had heavy losses in their counter attack at 5.30 a.m.	×Appendices 115 + 116
	Al. 2nd Liege Battery reported large number of German corpses seen lying between the trenches. Shells round about point B.× No hostile aircraft seen during the day – between 2.15 p.m. and 3.30 p.m. 8 Bristol and 1 French aeroplane were seen.	
	Narrative of principle events attached	× Appendix 120
	Copies of Reports by Colonel A. BROWNLEE, B.M. Battery R.3.A. and Captn. T.H. POYAH, 440th Battery R.3.A. are attached, also by O.A. 9th Bde R.3.A.	* Appendix 121
		MQS

WAR DIARY or INTELLIGENCE SUMMARY

Army Form C. 2118.

Hour, Date, Place	Summary of Events and Information	Remarks and references to Appendices
13th March 1915 NEUVE CHAPELLE	Very thick atmosphere different.	
12.17 am	Report received from LAHORE Division. Report Artil. time 11.24 am of that line. FEROZEPORE and JULLUNDUR Brigades are being fallen back of that line. SIRHIND Brigade moves temporarily at depart of MEERUT Division, who will command the CHOCOLAT MENIER corner to our front of junction with 4th Corps. Artillery of the Corps will be under the o-kind of MEERUT Division.	
12.30 am	MEERUT Division No 33/11 re of centres cancelled.	
1.8 am	MEERUT Division much to man all batteries to the particulars notified at about the hour before daylight - repeated to LAHORE Divisional Artillery and communicated no 4th Corps	
6.24 am	9th Brigade R.F.A. reported all quiet on their front - no attack.	
7 am	All R.A. units informed that no others yet received - offensive measures temporarily postponed - MEERUT Division plus the SIRHIND Brigade appears to be again taken as one the line and ordered to notes point and report developments.	
7.10 am	2nd Battery R.F.A. fired on 3 farms in M.3¹.2.9. by request of G.O.C. SIRHIND Brigade.	× appendix 123
7.11 am	2nd Heavy Battery reported hones in S.11 & 2.6 been entrenched and a lot of + to communication trench running thence to M.N S.E of K × - proposed to shelling this point as informed. In certain our troops had not reached it. meanwhile firing at probable observation station about 400 yds NE of DISTILLERY corner over area under observe. On Artillery opportunity	× appendix 115 & 116

WAR DIARY or INTELLIGENCE SUMMARY

(Erase heading not required.)

Army Form C. 2118.

Hour, Date, Place	Summary of Events and Information	Remarks and references to Appendices
7 am. 13th March 1915. VIEILLE CHAPELLE	Siege Battery near ordered to shell area to N.W. of where was commencement of both LAHORE and MEERUT Brigades. Also No 1 Group Heavy Artillery who was asked to turn "MOTHER" on to the group of houses in J.11 & 2.6 which would be a serious obstacle to our advance if not to be overcome otherwise. Siege Battery R.G.A. reported all quiet – our infantry apparently strengthening their position during night.	Q.2 Hour?
8.15 am. do	Observing Officer of 4th Brigade R.F.A. with SIRHIND Brigade reported Germans holding line also J. Oncor LAYES from S.5 to 3.6 to N.E. H.L.I. hold trenches North of the Oncor running S.W. Germans bombing H.L.I. heavily and G.O.C. wants Germans trenches shelled as far as safely allowed – a guessing distance which separates trenches before causing orders. Siege Battery shelled houses about 200 yds to N.E. of Duchkey Crow Roads (reported observer's steps) on shells PORT ARTHUR failed to hit it but burnt a lot of Germans out of it.	+Appendices 115 + 116
9.10 am. do	Information received from MEERUT Group. Report states own infantry are in advance to consolidate newly captured trenches shelled by enemy but trenches not reported. Reports also received that enemy has received good reinforcements.	×Appendix 123
9.23 am. do	Howitzer Battery reported they had fired at trench and house N S.11 × 2.6 at P.A.R. considerable damage done. Eye turn and 18pr. Battery also fired on this trench.	
9.30 am. do	Forward observing officer reported at 8.15am that we had the Oncor LAYES and are & railway through (sheet 34 ½) rough to the running 100 yds n. South S.5d to point M × BOIS du BIEZ. Enemy holding from next xxxxx .... C.R.A. & Heavy Artillery Informed that if shot correct it could not be safely shelled M.×	

WAR DIARY
or
INTELLIGENCE SUMMARY.
(Erase heading not required.)

Army Form C. 2118.

Hour, Date, Place		Summary of Events and Information	Remarks and references to Appendices
9.40 a.m. 13th March 1915. VIELLE CHAPELLE		1st Divisional Artillery were informed that enemy battery (located at S.21.a* G.1. by guns at Plenois) which enfiladed our trenches yesterday and caused much inconvenience. 1st Divisional Artillery reported at 10.5 a.m. that they would endeavour to knock out enemy battery with field guns. Heavy guns & their zone under Army orders.	*Appendices 115 & 116
10 a.m.	do.	14th Battery R.F.A. reports German field battery started shelling the RUE du BOIS and the O.P. from direction of DISTILLERY – shell falls S.W. of the DISTILLERY with a few shells.	
10.17 a.m.	do.	O.C. MEERUT Division informed C.R.A. that he wished heavy guns to engage trench guns that were shelling NEUVE CHAPELLE heavily. Col. No 1 Gp of Heavy Artillery asked to comply – no information re direction.	× appendix 123
10.40 a.m.	do.	14th Battery R.F.A. reports Germans are going into houses W. of BOIS du BIEZ – shelled the houses in conjunction with 440 How. Battery.	
10.47 a.m.	do.	All O.A. units were informed of situation as it stood at 10.45 a.m. as follows:– "BAREILLY Brigade hold from southern limit of Lahore Corps front to PORT ARTHUR inclusive with Brigade H.Qrs at RICHEBOURG. GARAHWAL Bde hold from PORT ARTHUR exclusive to NEUVE CHAPELLE with Brigade Head Qrs at AI Rebats. Square S3 x 6.3 – DEHRA DUN Brigade in support of RICHEBOURG S.VAANT and JEHIND Bde in support at NEUVE CHAPELLE. FEROZEPURE and JULLUNDUR* Brigades had been withdrawn to rear. 23rd Gurkhas hold line T.P.* B.* Londe bag collected at D* & 1/39th Garhwalis were at D* Bt N°1 Reinforcing tie on road through C* Group also informed of above situation also that it was quite safe to tell M*"	

WAR DIARY or INTELLIGENCE SUMMARY

Army Form C. 2118.

Hour, Date, Place	Summary of Events and Information	Remarks and references to Appendices
11.15 a.m. 13th March 1915. VIEILLE CHAPELLE	Arr. horse at S.11.b.3.6.	
	Report received from Black Watch through advanced observer 66th Battery and 4th Brigade that front de BIEZ S.12.c.3.8. full of enemy early this morning. Black Watch hold PORT ARTHUR and N.o.5 CRESCENT. Our line along RUE du BOIS continued by 39th Rifles and the Dogras. Reported to O.C. N.o.1 Group Heavy Artillery.	
11.23 a.m. do	9th Brigade R.F.A. reports gun at road junction 200 yds S.W. of Point X and having swung 300 yards E. of Point P* which could be observed from Point R.* 13th Brigade R.F.A. was informed of this. O.C. N.o.1 Group has asked if MOTHER could lay one 9.2. b. the gun.	*Appendices 115 +116
12.10 p.m. do	20th Battery R.F.A. fired a few H.E. into houses S.5.d.5.6. and 28.* Battery at Ft. de BIEZ.	
12.55 p.m. do	13th Brigade R.F.A. reports that advanced observer's officer at 12.30 p.m. says enemy reported collecting on & by-way our front - especially in bend in the L. River LAYES S.5.b. to M.36.a - 4th and 9th Brigades were informed of this.	*Appendix 123
1 p.m. do	7th Battery R.F.A. fired on section of enemy's battery in action S.W. of S.6.a.5.10 - enemy battery ceased firing - no direct hit observed - detachments seen running to cover.	
1.17 p.m. do	9th Brigade R.F.A. reported vicinity of Point D* being shelled by 5.9 hr. vzs. N.o.1 Group Heavy Artillery informed.	

Army Form C. 2118.

WAR DIARY
or
INTELLIGENCE SUMMARY.
(Erase heading not required.)

Instructions regarding War Diaries and Intelligence Summaries are contained in F.S. Regs., Part II. and the Staff Manual respectively. Title pages will be prepared in manuscript.

Hour, Date, Place	Summary of Events and Information	Remarks and references to Appendices
2 p.m. 13th March 1915 NEUVE CHAPELLE	Reported from left of GARHWAL Brigade on our ¶ that enemy were advancing — 4th, 9th and 13th Bde. the informed. O/C No 1 Group Heavy Artillery who were asked to shell line W.*J.* and S 6 a 3.5 and S 6 a 3.8 and to put any spare guns on to BOIS du BIEZ. LAHORE Divisible Artillery was also informed.	+appendices 115 & 116
2.40 p.m. do	13th Brigade R.F.A. reported no signs of enemy yet observed. O/C No 1 Group Heavy Artillery informed.	
2.50 p.m. do	1st Brigade R.F.A. reported that Forward Officer in NEUVE CHAPELLE reported no germans returning to the area at 2.45 p.m.	+appendix 123
3.30 p.m. do	4th, 9th & 13th Brigade R.F.A. were ordered two minutes rapid fire on Eastern edge and behind BOIS du BIEZ at 3.50 p.m. no germans reported seen there.	
3.40 p.m. do	13th Brigade R.F.A. reported their Forward Officer reported at 3.5 p.m. all quiet and no schema of attack by enemy — many of our batteries opened on the firing unnecessarily. 4th, 9th and 13th Brigades R.F.A. ordered to stop firing there & dawn of 20. MEERUT Divn. also informed. 43rd How. Bde. informed of night tires as follows — one battery covers trenches opposite our Southern post with one echo on good months	+appendix 122
4.20 p.m. 4.40 p.m. do do	S 17 c — one battery on A* and K* — the two batteries on A* and R* — and road North East of A* and K* — to keep enemy guns and stop to fire a occasional round to keep working parties were beings. Trouble from that direction — so working parties were being employed in connecting up point B* with Crescent trench.	
4.45 p.m.	2 Siege Battery informed that night their would not fire north of point K* to post M* without gun actually on M*	

WAR DIARY or INTELLIGENCE SUMMARY

Army Form C. 2118.

Hour, Date, Place	Summary of Events and Information	Remarks and references to Appendices
4.20 p.m. 13th March 1915 / VIEILLE CHAPELLE	OC 4th, 9th and 13th Brigades informed that Infantry report enemy advancing from Western edge of BOIS at 4.30 p.m. and ordered to keep good look out and be prepared to open fire at short notice if necessary.	
4.55 p.m. do.	13th Brigade R.F.A. informed that might bring up to time edge of BOIS in BIEZ from S.5.7.±O.1 to S 6 a & b. 9.	× appendix 123
5 p.m. do.	4th and 9th Brigades R.F.A. informed that night lines up to time of withdrawal on rear range as that allotted for operation before No 12 of yesterday-phase. Withdrawal will probably be at 3 a.m. of it takes place.	
6 p.m. do.	[illegible line struck through] M.R.B.	
6.30 p.m. do.	4th and 9th Brigades informed that Brigades will not be withdrawn tonight. 1st Corps reported enemy moving on East of BOIS in BIEZ. OC No 1 Group Heavy Artillery also informed with regard to same. No 2 Group + Cav'y of attack.	× appendices 115 + 116
7.37 p.m. do.	Gatch of LONDONS reported at 7 p.m. that enemy forming up on two front - patrol informed a steam at foot at trench mg between points N× and B× 4th, 9th, 13th Brigades also OC No 1 Group Heavy Artillery informed, also No 1 Group, H.A.	
	A LAHORE Divisional Artillery informed, also No 1 Group, H.A.	
	13th Hon Bale & 2nd Siege Battery	
	13th Brigade R.F.A. reported that Infantry patrol reported enemy forming up opposite the line N× B× opposite PORT ARTHUR	

WAR DIARY
or
INTELLIGENCE SUMMARY.
(Erase heading not required.)

Army Form C. 2118.

Instructions regarding War Diaries and Intelligence Summaries are contained in F.S. Regs., Part II. and the Staff Manual respectively. Title pages will be prepared in manuscript.

Hour, Date, Place	Summary of Events and Information	Remarks and references to Appendices
13th March 1915 NEUVE CHAPELLE	OC 9th Brigade R.F.A. suggested that it would seem advisable to use discoloured sandbags for topping parapets in place of new light coloured ones as it was very probable that the new sandbags used by the Londons drew heavy shell fire on them again. It was also noticed how well the German trenches showed up for observation round NEUVE CHAPELLE through the use of white sandbags — RITZ who constantly shelled throughout the day by batteries probably at T 20 n × Enemy's artillery was my active during the day principally shelling NEUVE CHAPELLE and RUE DU BOIS — No hostile aircraft seen today - between 6.15 a.m. and 3.30 p.m. eleven British aircraft were seen. × Map showing positions of C.R.A's Brigade Hd Qrs and Batteries of the MEERUT and LAHORE Divisions at noon of NEUVE CHAPELLE 10th - 14th March 1915 attached Narrative of events of the day attached Note on methods adopted by Meerut Divisional Artillery for anchoring guns during "Neuve Chapelle" operations are attached	× appendix 123 × appendix 123 * appendix 124 o appendices 124 (a) (b) (c) + (d) *WWG*

Army Form C. 2118.

WAR DIARY
or
INTELLIGENCE SUMMARY.
(Erase heading not required.)

Instructions regarding War Diaries and Intelligence Summaries are contained in F. S. Regs., Part II. and the Staff Manual respectively. Title pages will be prepared in manuscript.

Hour, Date, Place	Summary of Events and Information	Remarks and references to Appendices
8 a.m. 14th March 1915. LOCON	The G.O.C. R.A. LAHORE Division took over command of the Artillery on the line from the G.O.C. R.A. MEERUT Division. Head quarters Divisional Artillery MEERUT Division proceeded to LOCON.	
6 p.m. do	The positions of the Artillery of the MEERUT Division were as follows:-	
	Headquarters Divisional Artillery — LOCON	
	4th Brigade R.F.A. — LA COUTURE	
	9th Brigade R.F.A. — RICHEBOURG	
	13th Brigade R.F.A. — LA COUTURE	
	30th How. Battery R.F.A. — RUE des CHAVATTES	
	110th Heavy Battery R.G.A. — LA COUTURE	
	Meerut Divl. Am. Column — PARADIS	
10.30 p.m. do	Information received from MEERUT Division (Message No. G.3344/12) that two 18 pr. Brigades of MEERUT Division are to be withdrawn tomorrow for refit.	Appendix 12.
11. p.m. do	LAHORE Divisional Artillery asked to indicate the two 18 prs. Bdes to be withdrawn.	
11.30 p.m. do	LAHORE Divisional Artillery intimated that 4th and 9th Brigades would be	

Army Form C. 2118.

WAR DIARY
or
INTELLIGENCE SUMMARY.
(Erase heading not required.)

Instructions regarding War Diaries and Intelligence Summaries are contained in F.S. Regs., Part II. and the Staff Manual respectively. Title pages will be prepared in manuscript.

Hour, Date, Place	Summary of Events and Information	Remarks and references to Appendices
9.35 a.m. 13th March 1915. LOCON	Message to LAHORE Divisional Artillery suggested (by General Anderson) that if tactical situation permits it would be more convenient to interchange 9th and 13th Brigades, and leave 40th Brigade R.F.A. in action - This was arranged vide BM No 125 autographs thereon.	*Appendix 126
11.10 a.m. do	MEERUT Division Message No. G.1531 received stating that one Brigade R.F.A. to contain, a second Brigade R.F.A. possibly and one Brigade strength on two, one battery will be moved from Indian Corps area to 4th Corps area when noted for - 9th and 13th Brigades informed accordingly.	#Appendix 127
		NK9
12.15 p.m. 16th March 1915. LOCON	*Message No. G.340/3 received from MEERUT Division that additional 18 pr Brigade would be placed at disposal of 4th Corps and that this would be the 13th Brigade R.F.A. from the MEERUT Division - Also that MEERUT Division had that proportion of D.A.C.	*Appendix 128
1.35 p.m. do	Message No. G.340/4 from MEERUT Division to O.C. Brigade and the then Battery Commander of the 13th Brigade R.F.A. to report to Headquarters 7th Division as soon as possible.	#Appendix 129
3.16 p.m. do	Message No. G.340/5 from MEERUT Division orders for 13th Brigade R.F.A. and proportion of MEERUT Divisional Ammunition Column to march ENE of BERGUIN today - orders soon to O.C. 13th Brigade R.F.A. and Divisional Ammn Column accordingly.	#Appendix 130

WAR DIARY
or
INTELLIGENCE SUMMARY.
(Erase heading not required.)

Army Form C. 2118.

Hour, Date, Place	Summary of Events and Information	Remarks and references to Appendices
3.30 p.m. 16th March 1915 LOCON	Through M 340/6 from MEERUT Division to dispatch 9th Brigade R.F.A. at orders of Divisional Ammunition Column to join 7th Division. Orders issued to Col's 9th Bde. R.F.A. and Divl. Amm. Col. accordingly	*Appendix 131
17th March 1915. LOCON	RESTING	*Appendix 132
do.	*Message received from MEERUT Division that Brigadier General, General Staff, 1st Army and Artillery Adviser 1st Army would hold a conference of C.R.A's and Artillery Brigade Commanders at Headquarters Divisional Artillery Meerut Division on the subject of Howitzers (?) use of ammunition	
18th March 1915 LOCON	RESTING. 4½" Bde. R/10 F.B. in echelon north LAHORE Divn. 9½" to 13½" Bde. attached to 7th Divn.	
19th March 1915 LOCON	RESTING	
20th March 1915 LOCON	RESTING	
21st March 1915 LOCON	RESTING. Fine bright day. Major R.K. LYNCH-STAUNTON, R.A. Brigade Major R.A. proceeded on 7 days leave of absence to ENGLAND	
22nd March 1915 LOCON	RESTING. Fine bright day.	

Army Form C. 2118.

WAR DIARY
or
INTELLIGENCE SUMMARY.
(Erase heading not required.)

Instructions regarding War Diaries and Intelligence Summaries are contained in F.S. Regs., Part II. and the Staff Manual respectively. Title pages will be prepared in manuscript.

Hour, Date, Place	Summary of Events and Information	Remarks and references to Appendices
23rd March 1915. LOCON	RESTING. Rain during the day.	MWQ.S.
24th March 1915. LOCON	RESTING do	
25th March 1915. ESTAIRES-LA BASSEE Road M14 b 5.0	Headquarters Divisional Artillery MEERUT Division moved from LOCON during forenoon and established at ESTAMINET at M14 b 5.0 on ESTAIRES LA BASSEE Road. The 4th Brigade R.F.A. proceeded into billets at RIEZ BAILLEUL and the 30th How Battery into billets at ROBECQ (vide Div Arty's orders) 1st HDRE	MWQS.
26th March 1915. ESTAIRES - LA BASSEE Road M14 b 5.0	RESTING	MWQS.
27th March 1915. VEILLE CHAPELLE	Headquarters Divisional Artillery MEERUT Division established at the BREWERY VEILLE CHAPELLE. MAJOR R.K. LYNCH-STAUNTON R.A. Brigade Major R.A. returned from leave.	MWQS.
28th March 1915. VEILLE CHAPELLE	RESTING.	MWQS.
29th March 1915. VEILLE CHAPELLE	RESTING.	MWQS.
30th March 1915. VEILLE CHAPELLE	RESTING.	MWQS.
31st March 1915. VEILLE CHAPELLE	RESTING. Brigadier General R. St. C. LECKY, R.A. G.O.C. R.A. MEERUT Division and Lieut. F.N. MASON-MACFARLANE, R.A. Orderly Officer and A.D.C. to G.O.C. R.A. proceeded on short leave to ENGLAND	MWQS.

M Aynol-Dunder
Major R.A.
Brigade Major R.A.
MEERUT Division

APPENDIX III

LIST OF HOSTILE BATTERIES OPPOSITE M E E R U T DIVISIONAL ARTILLERY
WITH THEIR TARGET NUMBERS AND MAP POSITIONS - 3rd MARCH 1915.

Target No.	Map Position	Remarks
21	S 6 a 4 6	
23	S 6 a 7 6	
8b	S 17 b 4 5	Active.
52	S 17 d 6 6	
52b	S 17 d 8 9	
46	S 18 a 4 4	Very active.
7a	S 21 d 9 1	
7	S 22 c	
25	S 23 a 4 9	
55	S 23 b 2 6	
55a	S 23 d 10 3	
55b	S 23 c 8 9	
6a	S 28 b 9 10	
6b	S 28 b 3 4	Very active.
32	S 29 b 9 4	
5	S 30 d 2 9	Very active.
34	T 14 c	
1a	T 19 a 1 3	Active.
1b	T 19 c	
1c	T 19 c	
43	T 26 c 3 6	
4c	A 5 b 9 5	
4b	A 6 b 5 1	
41	A 12 d 8 4	
17	B 1 d 5 5	
17a	T 25 c 9 4	
56	B 7 a 4 5	
4d	S 29 d 5 2	
	A 23 a 7 7	
20	S 5 d 5 5	
	T 15 c 8 8	
	S 18 d 7 1	

LIST OF OTHER OBJECTIVES:-

57	S 16 b	Plantation.
50	S 10 b 8 9	Pumping Station.
39	S 16 a 5 0	White House O.P.
51	S 17 a 7 4	Distillery(possibly guns in yard. Also O.P.)
8c	S 17 c 10 0	House(L G H in W).
53	S 21 c 4 9	Orchard.
54	S 22 a 1 9	School House O.P.
55	S 23 b 2 1	Red House.
26	S 31 a 9 2	House(Defended).
S.H.	S 26 b 8 8	Snipers House.
P.H.	S 26 b 7 3	Piquet House.
G.S.	S 26 b 4 4	House with Green shutter.
H.R.	S 26 b 3 2	House on right of shrine.
X.	S 4 d 6 3	Cross roads S 4 d.
X.1.	S 17 a 6 9	Cross roads S 17 a.
X.2.	S 24 c 2 1	Cross roads S 24 c.
M.1.	S 20 d 10 3	Trench gun.
M.2.	S 26 b 10 9	do.
M.3.	S 27 a 9 4	do.
	S 21 a 2 6	Lone Tree Trench.

APPENDIX III A

RESULT OF EXPERIMENT IN LASHING WHEELS CARRIED OUT BY THE 14th BATTERY, ROYAL FIELD ARTILLERY ON THE 4th MARCH 1915.

At 11.15.a.m. fired ten rounds as experiment with trail and wheel lashed to trees on either side of gun, trail scotched against sandbags with sunken trunk of trees behind. Platform for wheels- brick with half filled sandbags on top. At the first round wheels sunk one degree, the second 45 minutes, the third 30 minutes, the fourth 15 minutes, the fifth 5 minutes, the remaining five rounds gun did not move either vertically or horizontally and direct hits were obtained on a house at 4,000. House fired at square 3 6 d 7'4.

SECRET   Copy No. 8

OPERATION ORDER No 21.

APPENDIX 11/2

LIEUT;-GENERAL Sir Charles ANDERSON, K.C.B.
COMMANDING MEERUT DIVISION.

9th March 1915.

Reference Map:-
LA BASSÉE-BETHUNE 1/40,000, also
G.H.Q. No.589b issued herewith.

Information. 1. The 4th and Indian Corps are to attack NEUVE CHAPELLE on March 10th, with the immediate object of capturing the enemy's trenches west of that village and the occupation of a line to the east of the eastern boundary of the "diamond" round NEUVE CHAPELLE.

The general object of the attack is to enable the 4th and Indian Corps to establish themselves on a more forward line to the east, the eventual objective being the high ground from AUBERS to LIGNY le GRAND, with the object of cutting off the enemy's troops now holding the front between NEUVE CHAPELLE and LA BASSÉE.

The 8th and Meerut Divisions, reinforced by the artillery of the Lahore Division and Heavy guns, are to carry out the attack.

The Lahore Division will be in Indian Corps Reserve.
The dividing line between the 4th and Indian Corps is:-

Point where the dividing line between the squares "M" and "S" cuts NEUVE CHAPELLE - cross roads in NEUX S.6.a.6.9 - cross roads at LA CLIQUERERIE Fe.

The 1st Corps is assaulting the enemy's lines North East of GIVENCHY.

Intention. 2. The Meerut Division will as its first objective attack the German trenches extending from the front of PORT ARTHUR to opposite the left of the line held by the Meerut Division (C to H), and push on to the north side of the cross roads F.D., forming the base of the triangle with its apex at NEUVE CHAPELLE Village, till the line C.O G.H. is reached.

Subsequent objectives will be:-
(a) The best available line on the east side of PORT ARTHUR - NEUVE CHAPELLE Road.
(b) The eastern edge of the BOIS du BIEZ.
(c) Line through LE HUE and LIGNY le GRAND to LA CLIQUETERIE Fe exclusive.

During these various advances all commanders must bear in mind the necessity for being prepared to specially protect the right flank of the movement.

Artillery. 3. The artillery reinforced by that of the Lahore Division and Heavy Artillery, 1st Army, will carry out a preliminary bombardment for thirtyfive minutes commencing at seven thirty A.M. to destroy obstacles, defences and machine guns on the front to be assaulted, to render hostile observing stations untenable, and prevent arrival of reinforcements. Batteries have also been detailed to demonstrate against enemy's trenches on the RUE du BOIS front. The range and fuze will then be increased to cover the infantry assault at 8.5 a.m. on enemy trenches.

Artillery fire will be maintained on NEUVE CHAPELLE village M.35.a and c from 6.5 a.m. to 8.35 a.m. when the village will be assaulted.

Garhwal 4. The Garhwal Brigade will assault the enemy's trenches as in para 2. The assault will be delivered at 8.5
Brigade. A.M. The assault by the 8th Division on the village of NEUVE CHAPELLE will commence at 8.35 a.m. and the Garhwal Brigade will advance to the eastern boundary of the NEUVE CHAPELLE diamond in conjunction with the advance of the 8th Division on its left. It will form for the assault in PORT ARTHUR, Advanced Post No. 2, the trenches along the ESTAIRES - LA BASSÉE Road and in the two new lines of breastwork immediately in rear of them.

Report Centre S.3.b.5.2.

2.

Blocking parties to close all enemy trenches, and bombing parties to work outwards and clear enemy's trenches on both flanks, will be organised by G.O.C. Garhwal Brigade and will accompany the assault.

Dehra Dun Brigade. 5. The Dehra Dun Brigade will be in support and will be formed up in positions of readiness in work A.1, works D.6 and D.7 and the breastwork connecting them, E.7 and E.8 and E.9 and 10, and work about cross roads at St VAAST. It will move into the position of assembly in rear of the Garhwal Brigade and the parties of S. & M. and Pioneers mentioned in paragraph 7, and will be careful not to block any of these units.

As the attack progresses the Brigade will be closed up to the position occupied by the Garhwal Bde prior to the attack.

Report Centre, House M.32.d.8/4.

Bareilly Brigade. 6. The Bareilly Brigade will continue to hold the present line of trenches. During the artillery bombardment a heavy rifle fire will be maintained on the enemy's trenches, and the assault by the Garhwal Brigade will be assisted by heavy fire on both flanks. The progress of the attack by the 8th Division must be watched to avoid fire from our left flank striking it.

Troops holding the line from PORT ARTHUR exclusive to the extreme left of front hold by Meerut Division will be prepared to move forward to take over a portion of such new line as may be established by the action of the attack. PORT ARTHUR will remain garrisoned as a keep.

Report Centre - S.2.d.10/0.

Garrisons of PORT ARTHUR and Advanced Post No.2 will be withdrawn before the artillery bombardment commences and will reoccupy their posts after the first ten minutes of the bombardment has been completed.

The garrisons of the isolated advanced posts of sub-sections A and B on the RUE du BOIS Front will be withdrawn just before daylight, the line of resistance along this front being the Guards' trench, ORCHARD and CRESENT.

The houses on the RUE du BOIS should be vacated by all ranks during the operations as they will be liable to very heavy artillery fire.

Sappers & Miners & Pioneers. 7. The following parties will be formed under detailed orders of the C.R.E.:-
(a) Half Company S. & M. and two companies 107th Pioneers to assemble in the southern of the three lots of small breastworks "Z" close in rear of D Sub-section of the Bareilly Brigade Front.
(b) Half Company S. & M. and one Company 107th Pioneers to assemble in two northern lots of breastwork referred to above - "X" and "Y".

These parties, each under a R.E. Officer and equipped with necessary tools and material, will follow the Garhwal Brigade into their position of assembly and will be ready to advance when ordered to respectively put localities "C" and "D" in a state of defence.

Trench guns. 8. All trench guns will be disposed under instructions already issued to the Divisional Trench Gun Officer. He will hold eight of these guns at disposal of G.O.C. Garhwal Brigade.

Divisional Reserve. 9. The troops as per margin will be formed up under cover in vicinity of bridge over LOISNE River, S.7.b. and will form the Divisional Reserve under Lieut.-Colonel N.M.C. STEVENS, 107th Pioneers. One Company 2/8th Gurkhas will be sent forward to Bareilly Brigade Report Centre to take over prisoners when called for by the G.O.C. Bareilly Brigade.

4th Indian Cavalry,
1 Coy S. & M.
HdQrs & 1 Company
107th Pioneers
2/8th Gurkha Rifles
(less 1 Coy to be detailed for work under C.R.E.)

10.

3.

Hour of Assembly.	10.	All troops will be in position by 4.30 a.m. on the ~~day of attack.~~ 10th March.
Obstacles.	11.	Wire in front of our trenches will be cut and necessary bridges placed over ditches in front of our trenches, under orders of the G.O.C. Bareilly Brigade, under cover of darkness ~~in the early hours of the day of attack.~~ during night 9th/10th March
Medical.	12.	The wounded will be collected at the existing regimental aid posts in RUE des BERCEAUX (S.8.b and S.3.c.) Ambulances will be at VIEILLE CHAPELLE and ZELOBES. Line of evacuation along the Northern RICHEBOURG Road from RICHEBOURG St VAAST to VIEILLE CHAPELLE; thence via FOSSE onto the LOCON - LESTREM Road.
S.A. Ammn Depots.	13.	Depots will be formed as follows:- Garhwal Brigade close in rear of front line in Sub-section "D". Dehra Dun Brigade in Breastworks running Northeast from work A.1.
Prisoners.	14.	Prisoners will, in the first instance, be passed back to troops of the Bareilly Brigade who will hand them over to One Company, 2/8th Gurkha Rifles at the Bareilly Brigade Report Centre at S.2.d.10/0. Prisoners will be marched to LOCON from this point.
Aeroplane Report Centres.	15.	A station for receiving aeroplane signals will be established, near Bareilly Brigade Report Centre, at S.2.d.8.2. A station for receiving messages from aeroplanes will be established at R.34.a.3/8, near Divisional Report Centre. G.O.C. Bareilly Brigade will detail six men from 4th Royal Hrs as observers for this station, to be in position by daybreak on ~~the day of the attack.~~ 10th March
Traffic.	16.	The Asst. Provost Marshal will stop all civilian traffic in the Meerut Divisional Area east of the LOCON - LESTREM Road from 6.0 a.m. on ~~the day of attack.~~ 10th March + Ammunition supply vehicles from Artillery Brigade Ammunition Columns will leave the LOCON - LESTREM Road at X.1.b.7/0 and move via trestle bridge at X.8.a.10/5 -road junctions X.8.b.8/6 - X.4.a. X.4.d.4/7, then immediately west of LA COUTURE Church through R.34.b over PONT LEVIS at VIEILLE CHAPELLE; thence via R.33.b, rejoining the LOCON - LESTREM Road at R.32.d.1/8. Ordinary military traffic will leave the LOCON - LESTREM Road at ZELOBES and move Southeast to LA COUTURE and RICHEBOURG St VAAST by the road South of the LOISNE River. It will move Northwest by the road East of LA COUTURE and VIEILLE CHAPELLE to FOSSE where it will rejoin the LOCON - LESTREM Road.
Reports.	17.	To be addressed "MEERUT REPORT CENTRE" which is established at the White Chateau at Road junction west of hog-backed bridge over canal on Southern LA COUTURE ROAD, (R.34.a.3/8.).
Supplies	18.	Supply depots for use in emergency have been established at RICHEBOURG St VAAST and LA COUTURE for 6000 British and 10,000 Indian rations half at each place /D

CNOrr
Colonel,
General Staff,
MEERUT DIVISION.

Issued at 1.P.M. by Signal Coy.

(For distribution see page 4.)

4.

```
Copy No. 1 to Indian Corps (with map)
        2    1st Divn        do.
        3    8th Divn        do.
        4    Lahore Divn     do.
        5    Dehra Dun Bde   ( map in possession.)
        6    Garhwal Bde     do.        do.
        7    Bareilly Bde    do.        do.
        8    C.R.A. Meerut   do.        do.
        9    C.R.A. Lahore   (Map)
       10    C.R.E. Meerut   ( map in possession
       11    4th Ind. Cav    no map. 5 ℅ G b issued
       12    107th Pioneers  do.
       13    2/8th Gurkhas   do.
       14    A.Q.M.G.        do.
       15    A.D.M.S.        do.
       16    D.A.A. & Q.M.G. do.
       17    File.
       18 )
       19 ) War Diary
       20 )
       21 )  General Staff.
```

APPENDIX 113   14

SECRET.   OPERATION ORDER No. 10. Copy No. ....
                           by
Brigadier General R.St.C. LECKY, R.A., Commanding Royal Artillery, MEERUT Div.

Reference:-   1
Map FRANCE-BETHUNE 40,000.   8th March 1915.

INFORMATION.   1. The 4th and Indian Corps are to attack NEUVE CHAPELLE
                  on March 10th, with the immediate object of capturing the
                  enemy's trenches west of that village and the occupation
                  of a line to the east of the eastern boundary of the
                  "diamond" round NEUVE CHAPELLE.
                  The general object of the attack is to enable the 4th
                  and Indian Corps to establish themselves on a more forward
                  line to the east; the eventual objective being the high
                  ground from AUBERS to LIGNY LE GRAND, with the object of
                  cutting off the enemy's troops now holding the front
                  between NEUVE CHAPELLE and LA BASSEE.
                  The 8th and MEERUT Divisions, reinforced by the Artillery
                  of the LAHORE Division and Heavy guns, are to carry out
                  the attack.
                  The LAHORE Division will be in Indian Corps Reserve.
                  The dividing line between the 4th and Indian Corps is:-
                    Point where the dividing line between the squares "H"
                    and "S" cuts NEUVE CHAPELLE cross roads in S.8.s.6.0 —
                    Cross roads at LA CLIQUETERIE Fm.
                  The 1st Corps is assaulting the enemy's lines North East
                  of GIVENCHY.

INTENTION.   2. The G.O.C. Division intends as his first objective to
                  attack the German trenches extending from the front of
                  PORT ARTHUR to opposite the left of the line held by
                  the MEERUT Division.(C to H), and push on to the North
                  side of the cross roads F.B., forming the base of the
                  triangle with its apex at NEUVE CHAPELLE village, till
                  the line C.O.O.M. is reached.
                  Subsequent objectives will be:-
                   (a) The best available line on the east side of
                       PORT ARTHUR - NEUVE CHAPELLE road.
                   (b) The eastern edge of the BOIS du BIEZ.
                   (c) Line through LAYHUE and LIGNY le GRAND to
                       be CLIQUETERIE Fm. exclusive.
                  During these various advances all commanders must bear
                  in mind the necessity for being prepared to specially
                  protect the right flank of the movement.
                  The assault will be delivered at 8.....a.m. by the GARHWAL
                  Brigade supported by the DEHRA DUN Brigade.
                  The BAREILLY Brigade will hold the line at present held by
                  the MEERUT Division.

ARTILLERY.   3. The Royal Artillery MEERUT Division will carry out the
                  operations as already detailed verbally by G.O.C. R.A.
                  as in attached schedule.
                  Officers Commanding 8th and 11th Brigades R.F.A. will
                  each detail a telephone party under an officer to
                  accompany the Right and Left Centre assaulting columns
                  of the GARHWAL Brigade.
                  O.C. 4th Brigade R.F.A. will detail a similar party to
                  accompany the DEHRA DUN Brigade when required.

TRENCH GUNS   4. All trench guns will be disposed under instructions
                  already issued to the Divisional Trench Gun Officer.
                  He will hold eight of these guns at disposal of
                  G.O.C. GARHWAL BRIGADE.

VEHICLES.   5. The wounded will be collected at the existing regimental aid posts in RUE des BERCEAUX(S 8 b and S 5 c).
Ambulances will be at VEILLE CHAPELLE and ZELOBES. Line of evacuation along the Northern RICHEBOURG Road from RICHE-BOURG ST VAAST to VEILLE CHAPELLE; thence via FOSSE on to the LOGON – LESTREM Road.

S.A.A. DEPOTS.   6. Depots will be formed as follows:-
GARHWAL Brigade close in rear of front line in SUB SECTION D
DEHRA DUN Brigade in Breastworks running North East from work A.1.

AEROPLANE REPORT CENTRES.   7. A station for receiving aeroplane signals will be established near BAREILLY Brigade Report Centre, at S 8 d 2½–10'0.
A station for receiving messages from aeroplanes will be established at R 34 a 3'8, near Divisional Report Centre.
G.O.C. BAREILLY Brigade will detail six men from 4th Royal Highlanders as observers for this station, to be in position by daybreak on 10th March 1915.

TRAFFIC.   8. Ammunition Supply vehicles from Artillery Brigade Ammunition Columns will leave the LOGON–LESTREM Road at X 1 b 7'0 and move via trestle bridge at X 8 a 10'5–road-junctions X 8 b 8'5 – X 4 a – X 4 d 4'7, then immediately west of LA COUTURE church through R 3a b over PONT LEVIS at VEILLE CHAPELLE, thence via R 33 b, rejoining the LOGON-LESTREM Road at R 32 d 1'8.
Ordinary military traffic will leave the LOGON–LESTREM Road at ZELOBES and move South East to LA COUTURE and RICHEBOURG St VAAST by the road South of the LOISNE River. It will move North West by the road East of LA COUTURE and VEILLE CHAPELLE to FOSSE where it will rejoin the LOGON-LESTREM Road.

REPORTS.   9. Reports to Estaminet immediately W, of hog backed bridge at VEILLE CHAPELLE.

Major R.A.

Brigade Major, Royal Artillery,
MEERUT DIVISION.

Issued at 8.p.m.
By mounted orderly.

Copy No. 1   to General Staff, MEERUT Division.
"   "   2   to G.O.C. BAREILLY Brigade.
"   "   3   to G.O.C. GARHWAL Brigade.
"   "   4   to G.O.C. DEHRA DUN Brigade.
"   "   5   to G.O.C., R.A. LAHORE DIVISION.
"   "   6   to G.O.C., R.A. 8th Division.
"   "   7   to O.C. No.1 Group Army Artillery.
"   "   8   to O.C. 4th Brigade R.F.A.
"   "   9   to O.C. 9th Brigade R.F.A.
"   "   10 to O.C. 13th Brigade R.F.A.
"   "   11 to O.C. 43rd How: Battery R.F.A.
"   "   12 to O.C. 2nd Siege Battery R.G.A.
"   "   13 to O.C. MEERUT Divisional Ammunition Column.
"   "   14 to War Diary.
"   "   15 to File.

SECRET.   S O M M E I L L E.

OPERATIONS ROYAL ARTILLERY FIRST PHASE.

7.30.a.m....... 4th, 8th and 13th Brigades R.F.A. wire cutting. 50 rounds
per gun. Duration of fire 10 minutes.

7.30.a.m....... 2nd Siege Battery guns in selected points in S.6.b.

7.30.a.m....... 1 section 11th Pack Mountain Battery. Combined with CARNIVAL
Brigade in position of observation covering right flank of
attack.

7.30.a.m....... On trenches South of Right extremity of our attack 1 battery
43rd Brigade R.F.A. paying particular attention to work S of C
to continue firing without stopping until end of bombardment.

7.30.a.m....... 4 Brigade R.F.A. LAHORE Division forms a screen on 2nd Corps
trench in S.5.b, S.5.c till 7.45.a.m.
8 Brigade R.F.A. SAVORY Division demonstrate on enemy's
trenches on front South of RUE du BOIS bursts of fire as
required.

7.40.a.m....... On front to be attacked, 8 batteries 43rd Brigade and 2nd Siege
Battery; objective enemy's trenches. Duration 25 minutes.

7.40.a.m....... One section 4.7" guns on trenches N.E. of left extremity of
our attack for 25 minutes, then this section takes up duties
of a Counter Battery.

7.45.a.m....... 1 battery 4th Brigade R.F.A. MEERUT Division on trenches N.E.
of left extremity of our attack till 8.5.a.m.

7.45.a.m....... Remaining 2 batteries R.F.A. MEERUT DIVISION continue on
screen in S.5.b, S.5.c & 1 battery per Brigade engaging
groups of houses S.11.a.7.7, S.5.d.4.4, S.5.a.8.6.

OPERATIONS ROYAL ARTILLERY. PHASE 2. H.E.P.A.

8.5.a.m....... Field Artillery operations remain as in Phase 1, except 1
battery R.F.A. MEERUT Division on left extremity of our attack
which now goes to form part of screen
Southern portion of screen from point P follows line of
nullah trench running N.W. from house 100 yds South of N
thence to 50 yards South of point B.

8.5.a.m....... 1 battery 9" Howitzers on trenches in area:-
S.4.d.5.1, S.10.b.9.6, S.10.b.8'.8.5, S.11.a.1.8.

8.30.a.m....... Paying particular attention to point B till 8.30.a.m. when
it turns on to trenches in area:-
S.11.a.1.8, S.10.b.8.6, S.10.b.3.4, S.11.a.0.6.

8.5.a.m....... 2 batteries 4.5" Howitzers on trenches in area S.11.a.0'.1,
S.10.b.9.5, S.11.a.2'.5, S.11.a.3.6, S.5.d.4.1 and those
roads and houses S.5.

8.5.a.m....... 1 battery 4.5" Howitzers objective Redoubt S.10.b.6'.8 and
enemy's trenches in an area enclosed by nullah just W of
Redoubt BETAINES-LA BASSEE Road, front line of enemy trenches
and trench running S.E. to N.E. 150 yards W of Redoubt.

OPERATIONS ROYAL ARTILLERY. PHASE 3.

When our Infantry are ready to make their third bound
to former 2nd Corps trench the R.F.A. forming the screen
with the exception of the Southern Brigade lift trenches
their range and cover the road from road junction S.11.a.7.7
to S.5.d.6.4.
The centre 4.5" Howitzer Battery will turn on to road and
houses from point B to G.6 while the left 4.5"
Howitzer Battery will turn one section on to point K.

APPENDIX III

OPERATIONS BY ROYAL ARTILLERY MEERUT DIVISION - 10th MARCH 1915.

7.30.a.m. 3 Brigades Royal Field Artillery- Wire cutting from 7.30.a.m. to 7.40.a.m. A separate report on this operation has already been submitted. On conclusion of wire cutting R.F.A. Brigades formed a screen in front of our advancing infantry and commanded approaches to prevent enemy bringing up reinforcements.

7.40.a.m. to 8.5.a.m. 2 Batteries 4.5" Howitzers and 1 Battery 6" Howitzers bombarded enemy's trenches about to be assaulted; one battery 4.5" Howitzers at 8.a.m. commenced shelling enemy's trenches South of Right extremity of our attack to prevent reinforcements being brought up, and remained in action during the day, putting bursts of fire over this area at irregular intervals.

8.5.a.m. Remaining Howitzer Batteries switched their fire onto enemy's trenches in the areas allotted on South of our attack and remained in action during the day, firing at slow rate, mixed with bursts of fire as opportunity demanded.

3.p.m. From about 3.p.m. onwards 3 Brigades R.F.A. engaged western edge of BOIS du BIEZ to cover the front of DEHRA DUN Brigade which was formed up ready to advance on this wood. Frequent bursts of fire were ordered by forward observing officers and I am informed this procedure prevented the enemy massing on western edge of the BOIS DU BIEZ.

Night. Night lines were laid out to cover western edge of BOIS du BIEZ. Howitzers on areas described above.

During the day much information was received from the Artillery forward observing officers, which was forwarded at once to the MEERUT Division.

I am of opinion that much of this information was very valuable and those sending it are worthy of suitable recognition.

Brig General
C.R.A. Meerut Division.

APPENDIX 115

War Diary

Meerut D.A.

March 1915

APPENDIX 115

War Diary
Hecru D.A.
March 1945

APPENDIX 116

War Diary

Meerut D.A.
March 1915

18 PR
4.5" How
6" How

APPENDIX

APPENDIX 2

War DIARY

December 1914
Hd. Qrs. Divisional Artillery
MEERUT division

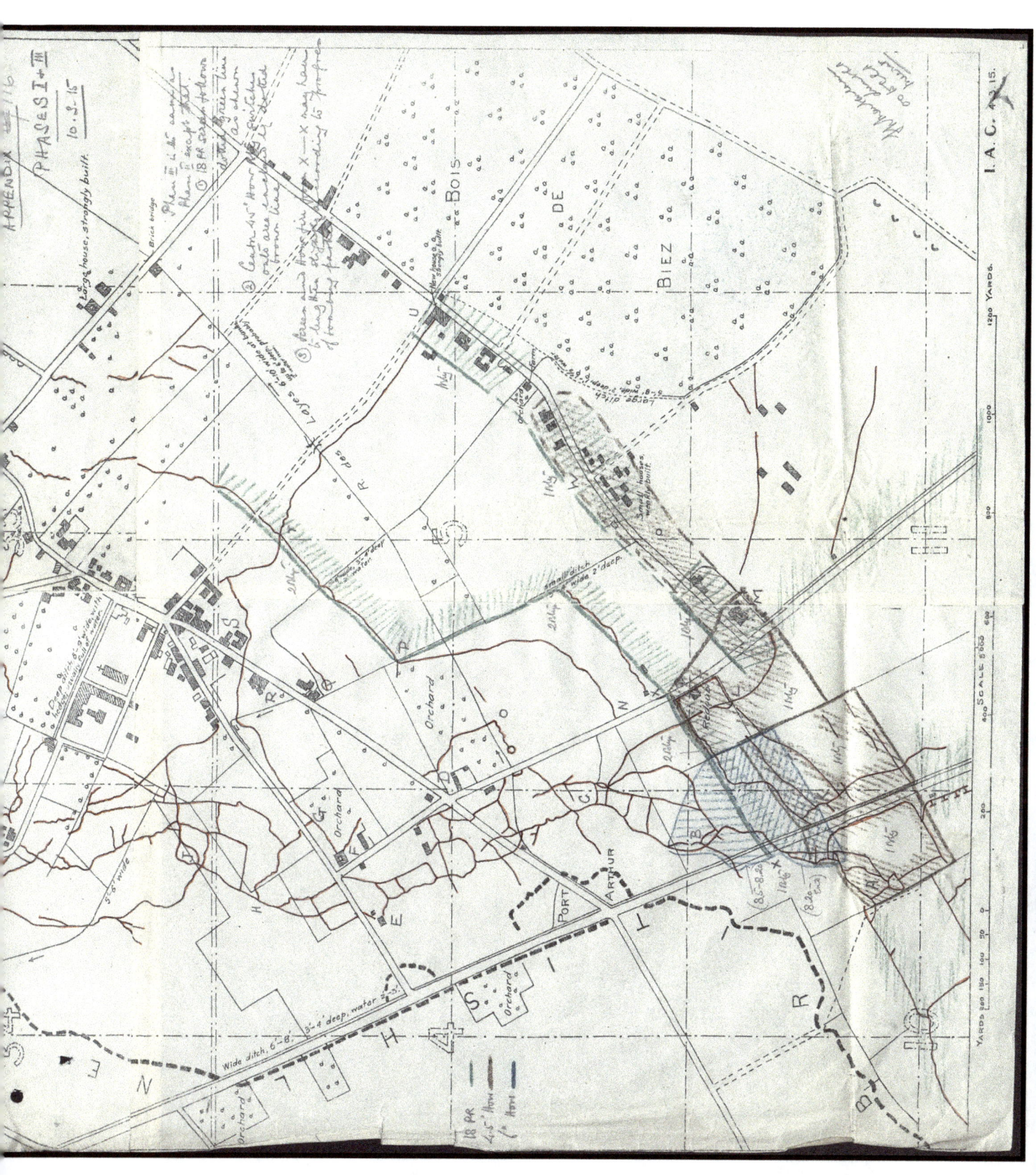

APPENDIX 116

War Diary
Mount-D.A.
March 1945

APPENDIX 117 COPY No. 9

OPERATION ORDER No. 11
by
Brigadier General R.St.C. LECKY, R.A., Commanding Royal Artillery, MEERUT Divn

References:
Map FRANCE BETHUNE-40,000 — 1 / —

11th March 1915.

INTENTION. 1. The MEERUT Divn with JULLUNDUR Bde and LAHORE Divn Arty and supported by No.1 Group G.H.Q. Arty will continue its advance at 7.a.m.
Objectives. BOIS du BIEZ, and then the line LA CLIQUETERIE Fe Rue(exclusive)-LIGNY le GRANDE(inclusive).
8th Division commences its attack at 7.a.m. as soon as its right reaches left of DEHRA Dun Bde the latter will attack BOIS du BIEZ on the front LES BROULET-LA RUSSIE as a first objective.
One Battn Garhwal Brigade will prolong the line on a front of 400 yds N.E. of road junction in S 11 c
BAREILLY Bde will continue to hold the line of trenches.

ARTILLERY. 2. 1st PHASE commencing at 7.a.m.
9th Bde R.F.A. will engage frontage S 5 d 0'3 to S 8 d 7'7
4th Bde R.F.A. do. S 6 d 7'7 to S 6 a 4'8 6

MEERUT Divn 13th Bde R.F.A.(less 1 btty) do. S 6 a 4'8 to S 6 a 5'8
ARTILLERY (in all cases inclusive)
1 btty 13th Bde as already detailed on houses in M 35 d 10'5, up to time of our infantry approaching same and subsequently on same area as remainder of Brigade. Ranges will be increased as the Infantry approach the wood.

LAHORE Divn 2 Brigades LAHORE Divisional Artillery for protection of Southern portion of our line from PORT ARTHUR to
ARTILLERY. CHOCOLATE MENIER Corner, and to guard approaches. Remaining Bde finds one battery on approaches in S 17 a and S 11 d. One battery on cross roads in S 12 c one battery in observation.

PACK ARTY. One section pack artillery grouped with DEHRA DUN Bde.
6" HOW: 6" How: trenches at point K.
1 4'5" How: on A.
4'5" HOWS: 1 4'5" How: on Redoubt 250 yds S.E. of A at S 11 c 6'8.
1 4'5" How on houses along road from S 11 c 3'5 to S 17 a 6'5. and on cross roads.

2nd PHASE.
As our Infantry enter western edge of wood MEERUT Divn Artillery will form a screen 200 yds E. of eastern edge of wood.
LAHORE Divn Arty 6" How and 2 4'5" Hows: as in Phase 1 or according to tactical situation.
1 4'5" How on LIGNY le PETIT.

3rd PHASE.
When our Infantry have made good the edge of the wood MEERUT Divisional Artillery will shell LIGNY le GRANDE to LA CLIQUETERIE.
Remaining Artillery as in phase 2 with the exception that the battery shelling LIGNY LE PETIT now shells HELPEGARDE.

Sd R.K. LYNCH-STAUNTON Major R.A
Brigade Major, Royal Artillery
MEERUT Division.

Issued at 4.a.m.
by motor cyclists.

Copy No.	To
1	General Staff, Meerut Division.
2	G.O.C., R.A., LAHORE Division.
3	G.O.C. R.A. Heavy Group.
4	O.C. 4th Brigade R.F.A.
5	O.C. 9th Brigade R.F.A.
6	13th Brigade R.F.A.
7	43rd Brigade R.F.A.
8	G.O.C. R.A. 8th Divn
9	War Diary.
10	O.C. 2nd siege battery

Note: The tasks allotted in above phases can only be accepted as approximate, they must depend very largely on the developement of the situation.

APPENDIX 116

OPERATIONS ROYAL ARTILLERY MEERUT DIVISION - 11th MARCH 1915.

The dispositions of the batteries under my command for 11th March 1915 are as detailed in my Operation Order No.11 (Copy No.1 in your possession)

7.a.m. The western edge of BOIS du BIEZ was shelled at 7.a.m. and the Wood searched; information was subsequently received stating that the attack had not been delivered by our infantry and

8.30.a.m. fire was asked for over this area at 8.30.a.m. Bursts of fire were ordered and fired at irregular intervals according as observing officers saw suitable opportunities.

10.45.a.m. A German counter attack was reported as being launched from N.W. corner of BOIS du BIEZ, rapid fire was turned on this area till German offensive was reported stopped.

2.8. to 2.12.p.m. The Infantry attack was ordered at 2.15.p.m. and the Artillery were ordered to prepare this with a rapid rate of fire from 2.8. to 2.12.p.m. on western edge of BOIS du BIEZ; this was carried out but the attack I understand was not launched. A slow rate of fire was maintained at intervals on BOIS du BIEZ, varied with searching fire.

Night. Night lines for protection of front were laid out - Howitzers on areas as described for operations of 10th.

During the day enemy's heavy artillery were very active. All such messages received by me were forwarded to O.C. No.1 Group Heavy Artillery to deal with, but owing to foggy weather I understand cooperation with our aircraft was not feasible and that the enemy's heavy artillery ran loose.

Sd R.St.C. Lecky
Brig General
C.R.A. Meerut Division

APPENDIX 119   Copy No. 10

OPERATION   ORDER   No. 12.
by
Brigadier General R.St.C.LECKY, R.A., Commanding Royal Artillery, MEERUT Divn.

Reference:-   1
Map-FRANCE BETHUNE 40,000
                                                        12th MARCH 1915.

INFORMATION   1. The Indian and 4th Corps will continue the offensive today in accordance with the general plan of operations already ordered.

INTENTION.   2. FIRST OBJECTIVE. The 8th Division will assault at 10.30.a.m. from houses M 35 d 10˙4 to road junction M 36 a 7˙10. 8th Division is responsible for capture of cross roads S 6 a 5˙9, and will then continue advance with Indian Corps. Indian Corps will assault and capture position from S 6 a 5˙9 to S 11 a 6˙7 at 11.a.m.
SECOND OBJECTIVE. Eastern edge of BOIS DE BIEZ.
THIRD OBJECTIVE. Line through LE HUE- LIGNY LE GRANDE- LA CLIQUETERIE Fme (exclusive).

ARTILLERY.   3. PHASE 1. 10.30.a.m. to 11.a.m.
9th Brigade R.F.A. will engage frontage S 11 a 7˙7 to S 5 d 3˙4.
4th Brigade R.F.A. will engage frontage S 5 d 3˙4 to S 5 b 10˙1.
13th Brigade R.F.A. will engage frontage S 5 b 10˙1 to S 6 a 6˙9.
During the period 10.30.a.m. to 10.50.a.m. steady "Searching" fire will be employed.
From 10.50.a.m. till 11.a.m. fire along the frontage named.
From 10.55.a.m. till 11.a.m. a heavy burst of fire will be opened on this frontage.
11.a.m. till 11.10.a.m. 4th, 9th and 13th Brigades (only) lengthen out and fire into centre of BOIS de BIEZ and on Eastern edge of it.

10.30.a.m.   ⎧ 2nd Siege Battery will shell houses at M and houses on road 50 yds N.E. of it.
to   ⎨ 1 4'5" How Battery will shell A and Redoubt 200 yds S.E. of A
11.a.m.   ⎪ 1 4'5" How Battery will shell K and the houses and trenches along the LA BASSEE road near K.
             ⎩ 1 4'5" How Battery will shell trenches between K and M and will also shell houses at cross roads S 17 a

10.30.a.m. to 11.a.m. LAHORE Divisional Artillery will assist by fire on approaches from the South and on centre of BOIS de BIEZ as arranged by G.O.C., R.A. LAHORE Division.

PHASE 2. 11.10.a.m. onwards.
The 4th, 9th and 13th Brigades R.F.A. form a screen from 200 to 300 yards East of Eastern edge of BOIS du BIEZ.
11.10.a.m. 2nd Siege Battery will turn on to Distillery Cross roads S 17 a and houses in that vicinity.
1 Howitzer Battery from task on trenches from K to M will come into Observation.
1 Howitzer Battery that was on A and Redoubt keep same under Observation.
1 Howitzer Battery that was on K and houses on road keep same under observation and also ground as far East as M.
11.a.m. LAHORE Divisional Artillery covers approaches from South and also roads in S 12 c, T 7 c T 7 d.
PHASE 3. After capture of Eastern edge of BOIS du BIEZ and previous to further advance MEERUT Artillery will shell LIGNY le GRANDE and BELPEGARDE and LAHORE Artillery the Southern approaches.
Howitzers Batteries to be in observation as in PHASE 2.

                                                    Major R.A.
Issued at 8.15.a.m.   Brigade Major, Royal Artillery,
by mounted orderly.   MEERUT DIVISION.

APPENDIX 119 Copy No. 10

OPERATION ORDER No. 12.
by
Brigadier General R.St.G.LECKY, R.A., Commanding Royal Artillery, MEERUT Divn.

Reference:-
Map-FRANCE BETHUNE 1/40,000

18th MARCH 1915.

INFORMATION
1. The Indian and 4th Corps will continue the offensive today in accordance with the general plan of operations already ordered.

INTENTION.
2. FIRST OBJECTIVE. The 8th Division will assault at 10.30.a.m. from houses M 35 d 10·4 to road junction M 36 a 7·10. 8th Division is responsible for capture of cross roads S 6 a 5·9. and will then continue advance with Indian Corps. Indian Corps will assault and capture position from S 6 a 5·0 to S 11 a 6·7 at 11.a.m.
SECOND OBJECTIVE. Eastern edge of BOIS DE BIEZ.
THIRD OBJECTIVE. Line through LE HUE- LIGNY LE GRANDE- LA CLIQUETERIE Fme (exclusive).

ARTILLERY.
3. PHASE 1. 10.30.a.m. to 11.a.m.
9th Brigade R.F.A. will engage frontage S 11 a 7·7 to S 5 d 5·4.
4th Brigade R.F.A. will engage frontage S 5 d 3·4 to S 5 b 10·1.
13th Brigade R.F.A. will engage frontage S 5 b 10·1 to S 6 a 6·9.
During the period 10.30.a.m. to 10.50.a.m. steady "Searching" fire will be employed.
From 10.50.a.m. till 11.a.m. fire along the frontage named.
From 10.55.a.m. till 11.a.m. a heavy burst of fire will be opened on this frontage.
11.a.m. till 11.10.a.m. 4th, 9th and 13th Brigades (only) lengthen out and fire into centre of BOIS de BIEZ and on Eastern edge of it.

10.30.a.m. { 2nd Siege Battery will shell houses at M and houses
to   { on road 50 yds N.E. of it.
11.a.m.   { 1 4·5" How Battery will shell A and Redoubt 200 yds
            { S.E. of A
            { 1 4·5" How Battery will shell K and the houses and
            { trenches along the LA BASSEE road near K.
            { 1 4·5" How Battery will shell trenches between
            { K and M and will also shell houses at cross roads
            { S 17 a

10.30.a.m. to 11.a.m. LAHORE Divisional Artillery will assist by fire on approaches from the South and on centre of BOIS de BIEZ as arranged by G.O.C., R.A. LAHORE Division.

PHASE 2. 11.10.a.m. onwards.
The 4th, 9th and 13th Brigades R.F.A. form a screen from 200 to 300 yards East of Eastern edge of BOIS du BIEZ.
11.10.a.m. 2nd Siege Battery will turn on to Distillery Cross roads S 17 a and houses in that vicinity.
1 Howitzer Battery from task .... come into Observation.
1 Howitzer Battery that was .... Observation.
1 Howitzer Battery that was .... same under observation and ....
11.a.m. LAHORE Divisional .... South and also roads in S ....
PHASE 3. After capture of .... previous to further advance .... LIGNY le GRANDE and .... Southern approaches.
Howitzers Batteries as in ....

No. 1 to General Staff, MEERUT
" 2 to LAHORE Divisional Art
" 3 to 8th Divisional Artill
" 4 to 4th Brigade R.F.A.
" 5 to 9th Brigade R.F.A.
" 6 to 13th Brigade R.F.A.
" 7 to 43rd How Brigade R.F.
" 8 to 2nd Siege Battery R.G
" 9 to O.C. No.1 Group, Heav
" 10 to War Diary
" 11 to File.

Issued at 8.15.a.m.
by mounted orderly.

Major R.A.
Brigade Major, Royal Artillery,
MEERUT DIVISION.

APPENDIX 120

OPERATIONS ROYAL ARTILLERY MEERUT DIVISION - 12th MARCH 1915.

Dispositions of the batteries under my command for 12th March are as described in my Operation Order No.12, of which you have a copy.

Indian Corps were ordered to assault and capture position at 11.a.m.

R.F.A. MEERUT were ordered to carry out bombardment from 10.30. a.m. to 11.a.m. with steady searching fire and at 11.a.m. lengthen out and fire into centre of BOIS du BIEZ and on eastern edge of it.

Above was postponed two hours and then carried out by R.F.A. Brigades

Later orders were received the position was to be assaulted and carried at all costs.

A bombardment on above lines was ordered and fired from 5.50.p.m. till 6.5.p.m. As far as I know in neither case was any attack pushed home.

Howitzers shelled selected points and areas as detailed in Operation Order above quoted.

Enemy's heavy artillery very active again on 12th.

All messages received were handed to O.C. No.1 Group Heavy Artillery to deal with, but owing to thick misty weather I understand observation from aircraft was not available, and again enemy's heavy artillery ran free.

Night lines for protection of front laid our by all batteries on areas ordered.

Sd R.St.C.Lecky
Brig General
C.R.A. Meerut Division

APPENDIX 121

REPORT BY 2ND LIEUTENANT A. BROMLEY, 8th BATTERY R.F.A.
12.3.15.

NEUVE CHAPELLE 8.55.p.m. The SIRHIND, JULLUNDUR, and 25th
Brigades attacked western edge of BOIS du BIEZ. As 25th
Brigade could not advance our own attack could not be pressed
home. Forward line evacuated by the DEHRA DUN Brigade last
night regained to-day by SIRHIND Brigade at heavy cost (H.L.I.
had 5 officers killed and 6 wounded) though their casualties
in the ranks were not unduly heavy. About 300 prisoners
captured to-day. I saw some crawl out of their trenches without arms and give themselves up. Prisoners report that the
men are starving and up to their knees in water.
When being marched back (all?) they came under heavy shell fire
from their own guns and dashed for cover in our trenches.
They report arrival of heavy reinforcements in the line in front
of the BOIS du BIEZ. They also say that the BRITISH rifle
fire is very deadly and the artillery fire is hell. Their
morale is bad and only fear from being shot prevents them
from not surrendering. Our Infantry are close to the river
LAYES and it is not safe to shell near it. This observing
station has been heavily shelled by 8" Howitzers all day,
but no hits have been obtained. Several small shell have
come in killing 2 men and wounding one.
NEUVE CHAPELLE could not be reconnoitred as a battery target.
The observing party was heavily sniped and came under heavy
shell fire as they came up this morning emerging with great
success. The orderly did a 100 yards carrying rifle haversack
and water bottle in 7 2/5 seconds. Everything is very
quiet now. Both 8nd and 44th lines are broken and telephonists
are out attending to them. Another attack is contemplated
to-night and ?? being in consultation now will advise
if Artillery support is required. Captain POWAH is reporting
to 44th Battery and to Brigade Headquarters.

REPORT BY CAPTAIN J.W. POWAH, 44th Battery R.F.A. 12.3.15

N 35 c 5'c. 3.P.M. SIRHIND, JULLUNDUR and 25th Brigades in order stated
from right to left attacked western edge of BOIS du BIEZ;
as 25th Brigade could not make progress the attack of
JULLUNDUR and SIRHIND Brigades could not be pressed home.
None of our Infantry are across the River LAYES but some are
near it, it is not safe to shell it. Redoubt at road junction
N 6 a 5's is reported to be giving trouble.
Fire of 44th Battery an S.E. half of front of BOIS DU BIEZ
about 5.p.m., was all plus and fuzed too short, height of burst
wants lowering about 10 minutes and range shortened at least
a hundred yards.
Parallel to road on N.W. side of BOIS du BIEZ and about 50 yds
from it is a German advanced trench which an F.O. Officer
reports that the Germans work on at night. He suggests that
this should be subject to an intermittent fire all night by
Artillery. I have not been able to see the D.V.C. yet as he
is busy but ?? telephone wires and O.O.C. wishes this done
I will call ??
From conversation with various Officers a gather failure of
attack was due to German machine guns and to some shrapnel from
British R.A. on our left from the flank of attackers.
I suggest sending all telephone wires of Brigade for this
advanced work i.e. 1st such battery line and to a Brigade
central ?? about ?? ?? ?? that stations in the
batteries being telephonists with relays of orderlies
half way houses for handing written orders & relays to relay
stations take ?? of shelling the road for approach
observer up at bty ???? and ??????? should receive
orders daily?

3. Presumably shrapnel burst on the flank of BOIS should be
??? their own Brigade????

REPORT BY OFFICER COMMANDING, 10th BRIGADE R.F.A.

13th MARCH 1915 - 8.30.a.m.

Prisoners captured in CRESCENT yesterday included Poles who said we were too good for them and very different to the Russians against whom they had been fighting the last two months. They were still under impression that they were within seven miles of PARIS. The 1st Seaforths did splendidly against "G" as it on parade. The Germans apparently cease to exist having done well right through. Prisoners state never had such an experience as our cannonading it was simply Hell.
It is confirmed that GILROY subaltern Black Watch was shot in stomach by a surrendered German.
Yesterday morning the Germans attacking against 7th and its Eastern vicinity in advancing over open were simply mown down by our maxims.

CIRCULATED FOR INFORMATION.

Major R.A.,
Brigade Major, Royal Artillery,
MEERUT DIVISION.

APPENDIX 122 6

Copy No. 6

OPERATION ORDER NO. 22.
By
Lieutenant-General Sir C...ANDERSON, K.C.B.,
Commanding MEERUT Division.

LA COUTURE, 13th March 1915.

Reference Map FRANCE BETHUNE 1/40000.

1. **Intention.** The Lahore Division relieves the Meerut Division in the front line tonight.

2. **Artillery.** Meerut Divisional Artillery, less 30th Howitzer Battery, will be relieved under arrangements to be made by C.R.As. Lahore and Meerut Divisions. Meerut Divisional Ammunition Column will continue to supply ammunition to the whole force, drawing on Lahore Divisional Ammunition Column. All demands on park being made by Meerut Divisional Ammunition Column. C.R.A. Headquarters LOCON after relief.

3. **Billets.**
   Garhwal Bde. Garhwal Brigade, (less 2/39th and 1st Seaforths (with added) will be relieved by the Sirhind Brigade on night 13th/14th, and will move into billets near ZELOBES. Arrangements for relief to be made jointly by Brigadiers concerned. Hour of completion of relief to be reported.

   Bareilly Bde. Bareilly Brigade will be relieved on the right section by Ferozepore Brigade under similar arrangements as above, and will march on relief to Billets at LA COUTURE.

   Dehra Dun Bde. Dehra Dun Brigade will move this afternoon to billets in VIEILLE CHAPELLE where they will be joined by 1st Seaforths when relieved from trenches. G.O.C., Dehra Dun Brigade will direct 2/39th Garhwalis to move into billets near ZELOBES to await arrival of Garhwal Brigade.

   2/8th Gurkhas. 2/8th Gurkhas, now attached to Bareilly Brigade, will, on relief, move into billets near ZELOBES as Divisional troops.

   4th Ind. Cavalry. 4th Indian Cavalry will move from LE VERT LANNET to billets south of cross-roads Q.28.d., which they recently vacated.

   S. & Ms. and 107th Pioneers. Nos. 3 and 4 Companies, S. & Ms. and 107th Pioneers will remain in present billets and temporarily at disposal of G.O.C., Lahore Division. C.R.E. Headquarters, LOCON after 8 A.M., 14th March 1915.

   Ambulances. No change.

   Train. No change.

4. **Command.** G.O.C., Meerut Division will remain in command of the line until 8 a.m., 14th March 1915, when G.O.C., Lahore Division assumes command.

5. **Reports.** Locon from 8 a.m., 14th March 1915.

C Norie, Colonel,
General Staff, Meerut Division.

Issued at 4 p.m., by Signal Coy. to :-
Copy No. 1 to Ind. Corps. No. 2 Lahore Divn. No. 3 Dehra Dun Bde.
       4   Garhwal Bde. No. 5 Bareilly Bde.   6 C.R.A. Meerut.
       7   C.R.E. Meerut   8 4th Ind. Cav.   9 107th Pioneers
      10   2/8th Gurkhas 11 Meerut Sig. Coy.   12 A.D.M.S.
      13   A.Q.M.G.   14 D.A.A.& Q.M.G.   15 D.A.A.G. 16. Train.
      17-18-19-20 War Diary & files.

APPENDIX. 123

Positions of CRA, Bde. Hd. Qrs. and Batteries of MEERUT and LAHORE divisions at action of NEUVE CHAPELLE 10th – 14th March 1915.

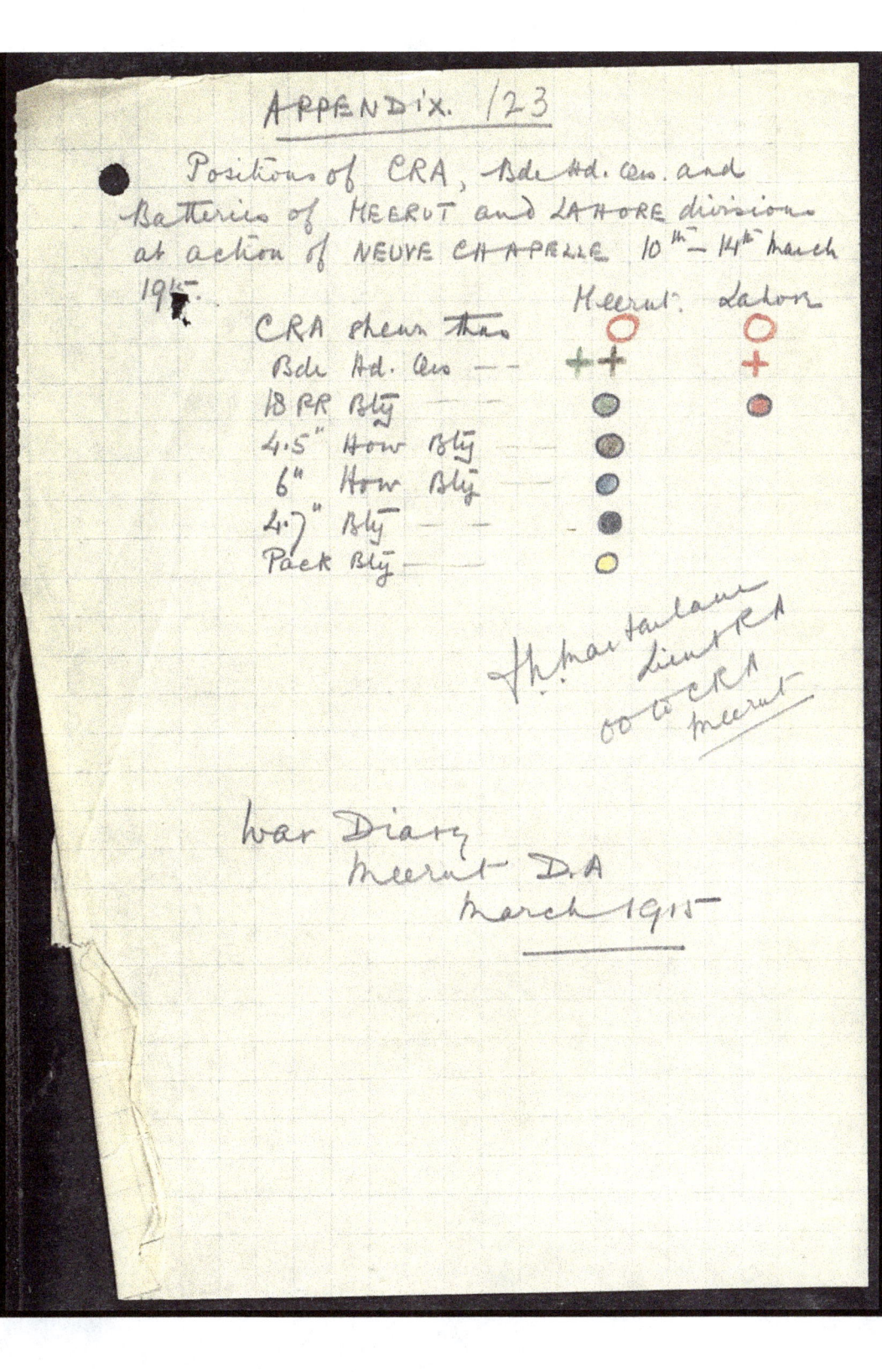

	Meerut	Lahore
CRA shewn thus	○	○
Bde. Hd. Qrs. —	+	+
13 PR Bty —	●	●
4.5" How Bty —	●	
6" How Bty —	●	
4.7" Bty —	●	
Pack Bty —	●	

J.M. Macfarlane
Lieut R.A.
O.O. to C.R.A.
Meerut

War Diary
Meerut D.A.
March 1915

APPENDIX 123

Note:-

This map has been cut to ~~economise~~ space — the squares outside the area shown will be found on same map which was submitted as Appendix 72 in a previous Volume (V.) of this Diary.

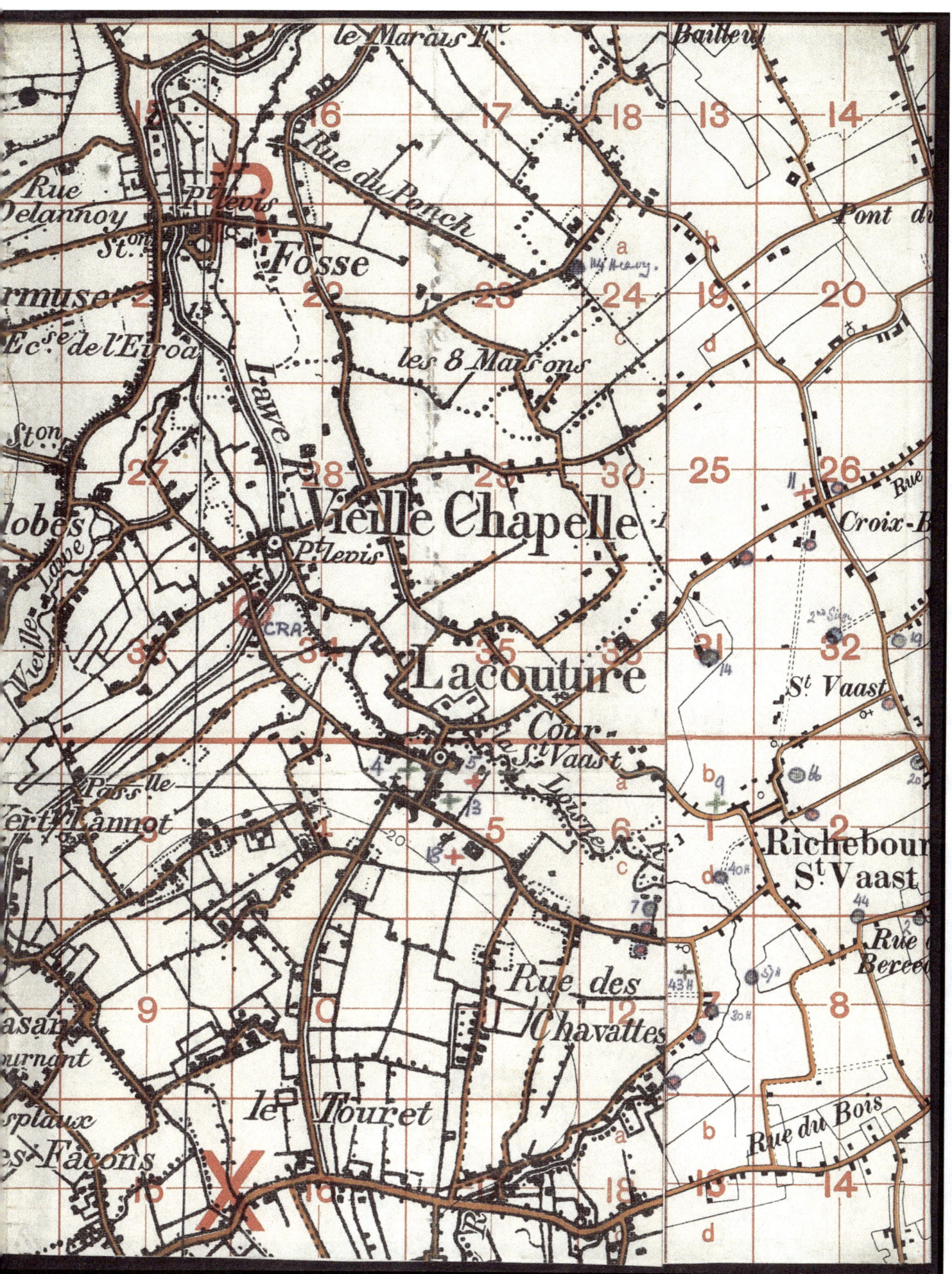

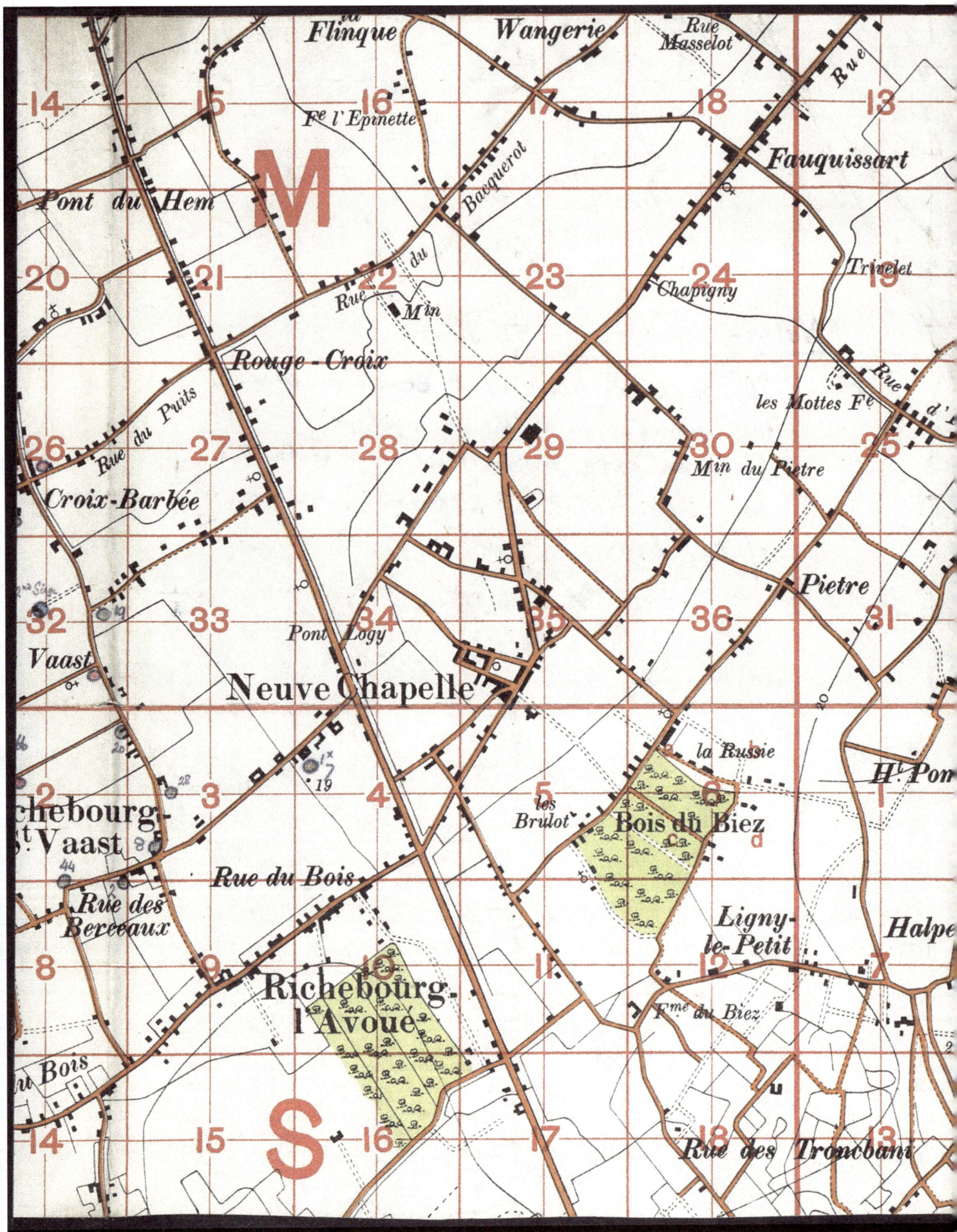

APPENDIX 124

OPERATIONS ROYAL ARTILLERY MEERUT DIVISION - 13th MARCH 1915.

On orders being received that the present line held was to be consolidated, the R.A. covered the front for the defence of the line, which operation was entrusted to G.O.C. LAHORE Division; Artillery being under command of C.R.A. LAHORE.

Sd R St C. Lecky
Brig General
C.R.A. Meerut Division

APPENDIX 124(a)

METHOD ADOPTED BY THE 4th BRIGADE, ROYAL FIELD ARTILLERY, for MAKING THEIR GUNS FAST DURING THE OPERATIONS OF THE 10th MARCH 1915.

Guns were not anchored. Gun platforms were selected of good sound substance as far as possible; the top layer of muddy ground being removed if necessary. Great care was taken to get wheels level. Under the wheels the best substance appeared to be hurdles, with sandbags scotching up and one sandbag partially filled under each wheel. This practically made the wheels immovable after a few rounds. Anchoring seems to be difficult to perform without a tendency to slew the gun one way or the other. A baulk of wood at the trail is useful.

         Sd L.A.C. GORDON, Colonel R.F.A.

2nd April 1915.   Commanding 4th Brigade R.F.A.

APPENDIX 124(?)

REPORT ON ANCHORAGE OF GUNS AND PLATFORMS IN CONNECTION THEREWITH –
AS CARRIED OUT BY BATTERIES OF 8th BRIGADE, ROYAL FIELD ARTILLERY
FOR "WIRE – CUTTING" ON 10th MARCH 1915.
––––––––––––––––

19th BATTERY R.F.A.

The ground where platforms were soft, hurdles or bricks were laid and rammed down and earth spread over them.
After several rounds had been fired, a balk was driven in and anchored behind the trail–(E.F.).
To prevent the gun lifting off the ground the wheels were tied down to pickets, front and rear–marked ●
To prevent movement front and rear and laterally the wheels were tied on to balks of timber.

[Diagram showing gun platform anchorage with points labelled A, B, C, D, E, F; Rear on left, Front on right]

AB, CD, by wire or cord, the balks being fixed by pickets shown ●
Lateral movement was also prevented by pickets ● driven in at the side of the wheels.

20th BATTERY R.F.A.

Similar to above, except that some of the guns which were on very soft plough had platforms prepared as follows:–
4 balks, 8" X 4" X 10 ft were laid down at right angles to the line of fire, and rested on three 8" X 8" balks.
The 4 balks on top were not flush with one another, but a space was left to allow stakes to be driven in, these stakes were used as additional holdfasts. Platforms were flush with ground level.

28th BATTERY R.F.A.

Gun platforms were dug out to a depth of about one foot, more or less, according to the ground.
The pit was then floored with whole bricks carefully laid, and then filled up with broken bricks and earth, well rammed down and made flush with the ground.
In swampy ground, a floor of wood balks was placed under the brick floor to distribute the pressure evenly.
The guns were anchored by lashing the drag washers and the ring on the front of the shield to pickets driven in in front.
A balk of timber was sunk in the ground in rear of the trail and sandbags placed between it and the trail to prevent the trail jumping off the wood–(to act as a cushion).
Sandbags, half filled, were placed in front and in rear of each wheel.
––––––––––––––––
It is necessary to fire not less than 6 rounds from each gun before anchoring, in order to allow the gun to settle well down on its platform.
Though all worked well, I prefer the platform prepared by the 28th Battery.

Sd FREDERICK POTTS Lt Colonel
Commanding 8th Brigade R.F.A.

1st April 1915.

APPENDIX 17

THE FOLLOWING METHOD OF ANCHORING GUNS WAS ADOPTED BY THE
13th BRIGADE, ROYAL FIELD ARTILLERY, DURING THE "WIRE CUTTING"
OPERATIONS ON THE 10th MARCH 1915.

1. **ANCHORING:-** Gun wheels were anchored from the front- stakes were driven in in front of, and slightly outside the wheels (see rough sketch). The rope passed from the stake to the felloes of the wheel, through the drag washer and thence through the trail eye and back by a similar route to the other stake. By this method the strain was taken by the whole carriage and not merely by the wheels.

    The carriage was also prevented from slipping back by means of a strong baulk, with sandbags in front, in rear of each wheel and also the trail.

2. **PLATFORMS:-** Guns were levelled as accurately as possible- platforms were made of either timber or bricks to prevent the wheels sinking.

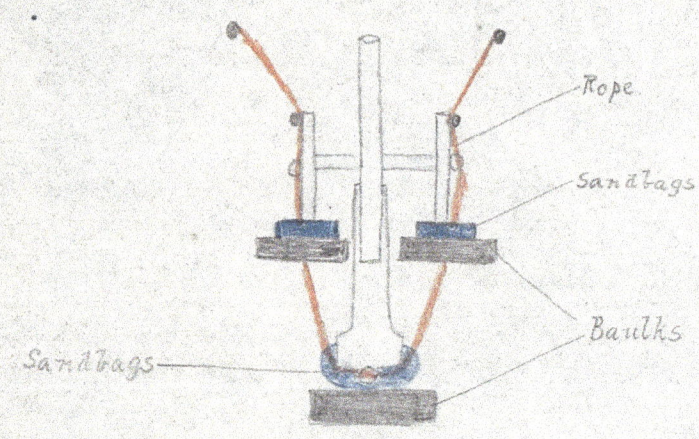

Sd H.E.J. ALVES, Captain R.F.A.
2nd April 1915. for O.C. 13th Brigade R.F.A.

"A" Form.   Army Form C.
MESSAGES AND SIGNALS.   No. of Message

APPENDIX 125

Prefix	Code	m.	Words.	Charge.	This message is on a/c of:	Recd. at	m.
Office of Origin and Service Instructions.					462 Service.	Date	
			Sent At	m.		From	
			To				
			By		(Signature of "Franking Officer.")	By	

TO { CRA

| Sender's Number | Day of Month | In reply to Number | AAA |
| G.334/12. | 14th | | |

Indian Corps wires begins G.179
14th Withdraw two eighteen pr
Bdes of the Meerut Divn from
action aaa hour of withdrawal left
to your discretion aaa Meerut Divn
to arrange billets in area allotted
in my G.124 so as to be readily
accessible if wanted aaa Lahore
Divn will indicate route to be
followed in its own area addressed
Lahore Divn repeated Meerut Divn
and Ind Corps 2nd Echelon. ends
for information

From: Meerut Divn
Place:
Time: 10.30 pm

Harlan
Major
GSO1

The above may be forwarded as now corrected. (Z)

"A" Form.   Army Form C. 2121.

MESSAGES AND SIGNALS.

APPENDIX 126

TO: LAHORE DIV ARTY

Sender's Number	Day of Month	In reply to Number	
BM 125	15	G 295	AAA

It has been suggested by General Anderson that if the tactical situation permits of it it would be more convenient if the 9th and 13th Bdes would be withdrawn and the 4th Bde left in action AAA This on account of the road from M 32 b to S 3 c being required for use by infantry AAA At present this is not possible as the guns of these two Bdes fire over the road at short range AAA Please reply by bearer if this can be arranged

From: Meerut Div Arty

9-35 a.m.

P.T.O.

for C.R.A.

II

Very well. The 9th + 13th B?? to be
removed. [illegible]

9

III

May the 9th and 13th Boles
be removed please, not the
4th? This on account of the Road
mentioned in I

[signature] Stamh?
Maj RA
for C.R.A. Meerut

IV

Quite alright — Unless
[illegible] he meant + meant
a chemical [illegible]
9 + 13 Boles are going
to LE CORNET — halt Q 27 —
[illegible]

"A" Form.   Army Form.
MESSAGES AND SIGNALS.   No. of Message_____

APPENDIX 127

135

TO: CRA Meerut Division

Sender's Number: G 1531
Day of Month: 15th

AAA

Intimation just received by telephone from Indian Corps that one Brigade RFA for certain, a second Brigade RFA possibly, and one Brigade Howitzers less one Batty, will be moved from Indian Corps' area to 4th Corps' area when asked for

Place: Meerut Division
Time: 11.10 AM

P Davies Major GSO

MESSAGES AND SIGNALS.

APPENDIX/28

149

TO: C.R.A.

Sender's Number: G.340/3
Day of Month: 16th

Indian Corps wires begins G.232 16th First Army Message 9813 begins reference last para my G.799 aaa arrange to place at disposal of 4th Corps an additional eighteen pounder Brigade ends Meerut Divn will send thirteenth Bde R.F.A aaa please give early intimation to me of destination of this Bde and Divn it will be attached to also routes to be followed aaa Meerut Divn will also send proportion D.A.C. Addressed Fourth Corps repeated Meerut Divn and Ind Corps second echelon ends for necessary action.

From / Place: Meerut Divn
Time: 11.45 AM

PRIORITY

Col
G.S.O(1)

"A" Form.   Army Form C. 2121.

MESSAGES AND SIGNALS.

APPENDIX 129

PRIORITY

TO — CRA

Sender's Number: G340/4   Day of Month: 16th   AAA

Indian Corps wires begins G235 send Colonel and three battery commanders thirteenth Bde RFA to report Seventh Divn as soon as possible AAA HQrs Seventh Divn is on road to SAILLY half mile East of where LA BASSEE — ESTAIRES Road crosses LYS River Addressed Meerut Divn repeated 7th Divn ends for necessary action reference my G340/3 of date

From: Meerut Divn
Place:
Time: 1-30 P.M.

Crorie Col
G.S.O.(1)

MESSAGES AND SIGNALS.

APPENDIX 130

PRIORITY

TO: CRA

Sender's Number: G 340/5 | Day of Month: 16th | AAA

Reference my G 340/3 Order 13th Bde RFA and proportion Meerut D.A.C to North east of BERQUIN today AAA Seventh Divn. arranging billets in square L nine Sheet 36 A one over forty thousand AAA Route HINGES - MERVILLE Road AAA Bde will send Officer to 4th Corps HQ MERVILLE to enquire for route beyond MERVILLE AAA Acknowledge

From Place: Meerut Divn
Time: 3-5 P.M

Major
GSO(1)

| MESSAGES AND SIGNALS. | No. of Message |

| Prefix | Code | m. | Words | Charge | APPENDIX 131 | Recd. at | m. |
| Office of Origin and Service Instructions. | | | Sent At | m. | This message is on a/c of: Service. (Signature of "Franking Officer.") | Date From By | |

PRIORITY

TO — CRA

Sender's Number	Day of Month	In reply to Number	AAA
G 340/6	16th		

Reference my G 340/1 Despatch ninth Bde R.F.A and Section D.A.C. to join seventh Divn today AAA Will march via MERVILLE—NEUF BERQUIN and RUE MONTIGNY to billets in square L10 D map one over forty thousand sheet 36 A ~~~~~~~ AAA Acknowledge

From — Seventh Divn
Place
Time — 3.25 P.M.

A Davis Major
G.S.O.(1)

MESSAGES AND SIGNALS.

APPENDIX 132

PRIORITY

TO: CRA Meerut

Sender's Number: G 1559
Day of Month: 17th

CRAs of Divisions and all Artillery Bde Commdrs are to meet Brig Genl Genl Staff First Army and Artillery Advisor First Army at Your Headquarters at seven thirty PM today AAA Please issue necessary orders and arrange for a room for conference which will last about fifteen minutes AAA Subject is expenditure of Ammn regarding which a letter No GS 58 D is being sent from Corps HQ AAA Acknowledge.

From Place: Meerut Divn
Time: 1-20 P.M

Col G.S.O.

INTELLIGENCE SUMMARY UP TO 11 p.m. 1st MARCH 1915.

I. HOSTILE ACTIVITY.

Field battery in S 18 c at about 8.40.a.m.

46 No.46 active at 8.25.a.m. but 2 rounds from 110th Heavy Battery quietened him.

58 b? A battery (not located) but thought to be 58 b, which shelled the RITZ at 2.20.p.m.

5 5 was very active during afternoon, about 5.30.p.m. flashes were clearly visible from the RITZ. It was firing in direction of LOISNE, is possibly a 15 cm. howitzer. Heavy snowstorm prevented it being then engaged by 2nd Siege Battery.
Battery at S 18 d 7'1.
4 field guns from RUE du MARAIS fired on front posts of 1st Division without effect.(S 28 b 3'4)
PORT ARTHUR was shelled at 8.30.a.m. and again at 11a.m. In both cases shelling ceased when 18th Battery opened with "gun fire" on German trenches. The fuzes of shell fired are of soft alloy of same colour as Aluminium- marked K Z 14
A B 14.

II. OBJECTIVES ENGAGED:-
BATTERIES.

46 46 by 110th Heavy Battery at 8.25.a.m. stopped after 2 rounds.
5 Battery at S 18 c engaged by 110th Heavy Battery at 8.40.a.m, by 2nd Siege Battery at 4.35.p.m. Effect appeared good.
46 46(S 18 a 4'1) also engaged at 11.30.a.m. by 8th Siege Battery. Observation from RUE du BOIS. One direct hit obtained- Observing officer reported fragments of material flew in all directions.
Battery at S 18 d 7'1 also engaged by 8th Siege Battery, with observation from same spot. Position from which flashes had been observed was successfully swept.
Battery at S 28 b 3'4 engaged by 35th Heavy Battery, observation by 2nd Siege Battery- Gun detachments could be seen. This battery re-opened at 4.30.p.m. was againe engaged by 35th Heavy Battery, 73rd Battery R.F.A. co-operating.

OTHER OBJECTIVES.

14th Battery R.F.A. fired at reliefs without rifles crossing barricade in S 5 c at 7.a.m.
Same battery fired at machine gun parapet at S 10 b 7'4, pointed out by Infantry at 12.p.m., also at party carrying sacks up communication trench in S 5 c at 5.p.m.
66th Battery R.F.A. registered iron plates thought to be M.G. shields located in pairs, one in fire trench in S 10 c and one in support trench S 10 b 7'2, the latter enfilading our front as far as CINDER TRACK.

III. INFORMATION.

Enemy working party was seen digging trenches in T 19 a and T 13 d.
About half company unarmed men was seen on road between LORGIES and BEAU PUITS at 3.30.p.m.
Three men seen in enemy support trenches in S 5 c dressed in Khaki similar to our own with brown balaclava hats.
More conspicuous white sand bags noticed in German parapet North of GIVENCHY ridge, clearly defining enemy's line.
No German aircraft seen to-day.
Much activity in Redoubt at S 10 d during day. An elderly lot of bearded Huns were seen carrying planks and sacks into it, some wore Balaclava helmets and others round shapeless caps.
Two officers in Grey Uniform with "brass tags" and rimmed caps visited the Redoubt yesterday.
When one of our shell burst near the Redoubt yesterday at 12.30.p.m. six men rushed out to collect "Souvenirs". The intention is to present them with some more to-day !!

Major R.A.

Brigade Major, Royal Artillery,
MEERUT DIVISION.

INTELLIGENCE SUMMARY UP TO 11.p.m. 2nd MARCH 1915.

I. HOSTILE ACTIVITY.
5. No.5 was active about 11.a.m. Flashes visible from RITZ.
52? A field gun in direction of LORGIES shelled the RITZ at 12.10.p.m., 2.20.p.m. and 4.30.p.m.
8b? 4 flashes were seen at 4.45.p.m. by observing Officer of 2nd Battery.
46? True bearing of 100° from his position gives a line running through 8 b and 46 exactly !
S 28 b 3'4 About 10.30.a.m. 2 field guns in S 28 b 3'4 opened fire as usual towards BREWERY. Flashes distinctly visible, and also numbers pulling the lanyard !

II. OBJECTIVES ENGAGED.
GUNS: Field guns in S 28 b 3'4 by 35th Heavy Battery, observation officers of 2nd Siege Battery observing, hostile fire ceased and detachments cleared away after 3rd round.
5. 5 located by flashes from RITZ firing from behind house at S 30 d 2'9. Roof of this house removed by 8th Siege and 6 rounds estimated as falling in the approximate position of this battery.
1a 1 a by 8th Siege Battery at 3.30.p.m. with wireless aeroplane and short bracket obtained.
OTHER OBJECTIVES:- Redoubt in S 10 d, effectively by 2nd Siege Battery. House in S 5 a 99(for registration) by 2nd Siege Battery, with aeroplane- Target 2nd round.
Cross roads in M 35 c 7'1 by 8th Siege Battery(for registration) with wireless aeroplane; 6th round set fire to house at cross roads.
4th Brigade R.F.A. Two batteries carried out registration from new positions.
66th Battery R.F.A. engaged Redoubt in S 10 d, observation by wireless aeroplane- results satisfactory.
Same battery at 2.a.m. shelled 40 to 50 men reported by Infantry repairing parapet, and stopped the work for the night.
2nd Battery R.F.A. registered M.G. emplacements in S 15 b 4'1 and S 16 a 5'0.

III. AEROPLANE RECONNAISSANCE (8.30.a.m. to 9.50.a.m.).
No new trenches could be picked out in T 19 a or T 13 d where digging was reported in progress yesterday.
1a T 19 a 1'3 Ground appeared much trodden in, in two oblong shaped yards adjoining and N. of the Church, which appeared only likely spot for guns. No flashes or guns actually seen.
51 S 17 a 6'4 Distillery yard appeared to contain guns also stacks of Beet or manure.
55 Objects which might have been guns were observed at S 23 b 2'6 or Cinder Track. Ground round about well trodden in. Nonfiring observed.
S 16 a 1'2 ---------ditto.---------
17a A battery at T 25 c 9'4 was noticed in small orchard by another airman yesterday. Will be known as 17 a

IV. ANTI AIRCRAFT SECTION REPORT:-
Two German L.V.G's approached from E. at 9.30.a.m. one to within 5,700 yds the other to within 6,500 yds. They turned round and fled when a B.E. and a MORANE approached them, without giving our "Archibald" a shot. The nearer one was over the BOIS be BIEZ(approximately).
German "Sausage" up near HOLLUCH from 1.30.p.m. to 4.p.m.
French "Sausage" up near VERMELLES from 2.p.m. to 4.p.m.
9 British and 2 French aeroplanes sighted.

V. INFORMATION. Red cross wagon seen on LORGIES-BEAU PUITS road at 2.20.p.m.(? collecting the "bag" from No.5).
Periscope seen in S 10 a-possibly O.P. for fire on "RITZ".
Flashes and smoke from enemy guns are reported as being much more conspicuous than formerly. Possibly deterioration of cordite accounts for this.
Much movement reported in German trenches in afternoon. A few of the men reported as wearing caps with Red head bands.

R.K.Lynch-Stambo Major R.A.
Brigade Major, Royal Artillery.
MEERUT DIVISION.

INFORMATION SUMMARY UP TO 10.p.m. 3rd MARCH 1915.

I. **HOSTILE ACTIVITY.**

46   46 was active at 11.40.a.m. and 3.20.p.m.
5   5 was active at 1.40.p.m.
52b   "RITZ" shelled at 3.p.m. by battery thought to be 52b. This battery was active again at 3.40.p.m.
      14th Battery Observation Post shelled from 3 to 3.30.p.m. All shells about 150 yards short.
      RICHEBOURG St VAAST shelled at 11.30.a.m.
6a   Two sections seen firing near S 28 b 8'4.

II. **OBJECTIVES ENGAGED.**
    (a) BATTERIES.-
46   46 by 110th Heavy Battery. Failed to silence him owing to lack of lyddite.
8b?   Battery in S 17 b by 14th Battery R.F.A.
5   5 by 8th Siege Battery.
6a   At S 28 b 3'4 by 2nd Siege Battery. Battery immediately silenced.
    (b) OTHER OBJECTIVES.-
      LORGIES by 110th Heavy Battery and 8th Siege Battery in reply to shelling of RICHEBOURG St VAAST.
      The following by 14th Battery:-
      Houses in S 5 d from which smoke was issuing at 7.35.a.m.
      Parties of enemy in communication trench in S 5 c at 8.35.a.m.
      Houses and road in S 5 b where small party of enemy seen.
      Houses on ESTAIRES-LA BASSEE Road reported as a probable Observation Post by Infantry in PORT ARTHUR.
      Snipers in S 10 b and S 5 c. Effect good.
      Germans carrying planks in communication trench in S 5 c.
      Machine guns in fire trench while our reliefs were in progress.
      109th Heavy Battery and 2nd Siege Battery carried out some registration.
      Redoubt in S 10 d 5'9 bombarded by 2nd Siege Battery and 7th Battery R.F.A. Part of parapet to E. and S. blown away.

III. **INFORMATION.**
Too rough for aeroplane work.
Several Germans seen in sandbag Redoubt S 10 b 5'1. Work was going on here with stakes and mauls. For about 200 yards S.W. of this point there is no wire in front of the german fire trench but further on as far as the trench N. of 39 the wire is very thick and the trench apparently unoccupied.
The Germans seen had red bands round their caps.
Considerable work has been done, generally, on front line breastworks from LONE TREE TRENCH to the SHRINE.
6a (located at S 28 b 3'4) has two sections in action and uses black powder giving distinct puffs of smoke. The sections are close together but fire in different directions. The guns of the right section are behind a haystack and a house respectively.
Detachments were seen going to and fro.
There is a possible M.G. emplacement at S 10 c 4'5.
A small bastion is being prepared at S 10 c 2'3.
Between these two points the parapet is being strengthened and repaired with sandbags.
During registration of Redoubt S 10 d 5'9 by 2nd Siege Battery on 2nd February 1915 a lot of wire entanglement was blown up.

                                        F.MacFarlane, Lieut R.A.
                                        for Major R.A.,
                                  Brigade Major, Royal Artillery,
                                         MEERUT DIVISION.

INTELLIGENCE SUMMARY UP TO 11.30.p.m. 4th MARCH 1915.

I. **HOSTILE ACTIVITY**-
Hostile guns very much more active during the day than they have been for some time past. This was almost entirely confined to their Howitzers. Their objective apparently houses along RUE du BOIS from cross roads S 9 d 1'7 and S 10 a 9'9.

46   46 was active at 1.p.m. and at 3.30.p.m.
      The RITZ and RUE du BOIS shelled 8.30. to 9.a.m. also at 10.5.a.m., 12.35.p.m. and 2.30.p.m. by a 15 c.m. howitzer and also a field battery. Flashes not located but supposed bearing of 130° (true)
17a(?) would run through 17a(?) One flash was observed S. of 1a's position-
1a(?) possibly 1b(T 19 b).
8a   8a(or 8b)(S 28 b 3'4) active at 12.45 and 3.p.m. towards houses "A" and "B" until silenced by 2nd Siege Battery.
5   5 was thought to be active at 10.35.a.m.

II. **OBJECTIVES ENGAGED**.

8a or GUNS:- 8a or 8b(S 28 b 0'4) by 8th Siege Battery, two hits obtained
8b   on battery.
5   5 registered by 2nd Siege Battery.
46   46 registered by 2nd Siege Battery.
       OTHER OBJECTIVES:- Redoubt and neighbouring trenches in S 10 b 6'5 registered by 30th Howitzer Battery.
       VIOLAINES registered by 8th Siege Battery.
       WHITE HOUSE treated with shrapnel by 110th Heavy Battery as supposed O.P.
       7th Battery fired on M.G. in trench S 4 b 5'7., and on snipers house S 4 b 8'4.
       14th Battery fired on Redoubt S 10 b 6'5 and on enemy carrying sand bags along communicating trench.

III. **ANTI-AIRCRAFT REPORT**.
No German aeroplanes seen today.
Two German "Saussges" went up, one at 7.30.a.m. and the other at 10.a.m. They were very close together about 15,000 yards SSE of LA COUTURE. They descended at 2.p.m.
A French "Sausage" went up about 7.30.a.m. about 12,000 yards S. of LA COUTURE and remained up until 1.p.m.
Several British and French aeroplanes about from 7.30.a.m. till ?

IV. **INFORMATION**:
There are two dummy guns under an embankment a little North of VIOLAINES Distillery, position S 30 c 8'1(Approx). Emplacements of Nos.23 and 40 also both contain a section of dummy guns.
New dark grey uniform seen in enemy trenches, with peaked cap-black peak.
A steady daily strengthening of all breastworks and redoubts reported from BREWERY.
It is suggested that the periscope in S 10 a observes fire on this section.
Redoubt in S 16 a.- Parts of the parapet are 4 to 6 feet high and appear to be as thick. Tops heavily sandbagged and rear portions revetted with hurdles. A certain amount of baling noticed there this morning.
Along hostile front trench from S 10 c to S 10 b where parapet has been heightened and built up with sand bags, wooden loopholes have been replaced by steel plates, loopholes in which are shuttered.
Between 11.30.a.m. and 12 noon some activity noticed about S 10 c, a party of 10 or 12 men hauling at some object invisible from RITZ. In this neighbourhood short white stakes are noticeable- possibly marking out a line of trench work.
2.15.p.m. A party of 40 or 50 unarmed men were seen marching from VIOLAINES via BEAU puits to LOGIES.
Most of the above information furnished by Observation Officer of 2nd Siege Battery.
From the Barricade on the road S 10 b 7'7 to about 200 yds N.E. the parapet is reported as very small, with practically no wire.
An interesting report of experiments carried out by O.C. 14th Battery during the day, by lashing gun wheels, is being circulated separately.

Major R A
Brigade Major Royal Artillery,
MEERUT DIVISION.

INTELLIGENCE SUMMARY UP TO 11.p.m. 8th MARCH 1915.

I. HOSTILE ACTIVITY.
On the whole the German Artillery was not so active
along the RUE du BOIS to-day.

46   4G was reported active by 110th Heavy Battery at J.26.D.4.
23?)A battery E. of NEUVE CHAPELLE shelled vicinity of RICHEBOURG
81?)during afternoon.
61   Guns at DISTILLERY shelled PORT ARTHUR at 2.15.p.m.

II. OBJECTIVES ENGAGED.
7th Battery, R.F.A. carried out registration of enemy trenches.
11th Battery R.F.A. registered on orchard. Shelled ruined
house S.12.a.2'8 reported by Infantry to shelter enemy observer,
and repeated this operation every time German Howitzer opened
fire.
26th Battery R.F.A. fired on Observation House S.10 & b.6 at
1.10.p.m. fired on working party in Redoubt S.10.d.
2nd Battery registered Red House Farm S.16.a.o'6.
36th Howitzer Battery registered on Redoubt S.10.b.6'1, barricade
S.12.b.7'7, houses at road junction S.11.d. Redoubt in S.a.d.10'4.
Gap in enemy trench S.4.d.8'3. which extended for 50 yards- no
wire visible.
2nd Siege Battery registered House in S.a.b.5/6- DEAD COW FARM
and other points.

III. INFORMATION.
An Infantry Officer took "scrap" bearings of two shells which
fell in S.a.c. which indicated the E. of LORGIES.
O.C. 36th Howitzer Battery reports a new 12 c.m. Howitzer was
registering the RUE du BOIS yesterday.

NOTE:-   Further information is required of positions of enemy's
         Redoubts and Machine Guns.

                                        signature
                                        Major R.A.,

                                Brigade Major, Royal Artillery,
                                MEERUT DIVISION.

INTELLIGENCE SUMMARY UP TO 10.p.m. 6th March 1915.

I. HOSTILE ACTIVITY.

46. 46 reported active at 11.7.a.m. by 110th Heavy Battery.
A battery at LORGIES (flashes invisible) opened fire on RICHEBOURG at 4.5.p.m.
RUE du BOIS O.P. shelled at 2.30.p.m. and 3.p.m. from direction of DISTILLERY.
PONT LOGY was shelled at 11.30.a.m.

II. OBJECTIVES ENGAGED.
Fire chiefly confined to possible O.P's and to carrying out registration.
(6.p.m. 5.3.15.) 14th Battery fired several effective rounds on party of 60 Germans leaving fire trench via Redoubt S 10 b.
66th Battery fired a few rounds at enemy's pump where large quantities of water was being drawn out at 9.30.a.m.

III. INFORMATION.
Heavy firing heard to the North at 4.30.a.m.
3.25.p.m. fairly heavy gun and rifle fire heard towards FESUIBERT.
An Infantry officer considers from personal observation that the battery which shells RUE du BOIS daily is located behind a hedge in square S 23 c 9'4.

[signature: O.M. Lynch-Staunton]

Major R.A.,

Brigade Major, Royal Artillery,
MEERUT DIVISION.

INTELLIGENCE SUMMARY UP TO 11 p.m. 7th MARCH 1915.

I. HOSTILE ACTIVITY.
"PIPSQUEAK" fired on road S 3 b at 9.50.a.m.
52. 52 was active at 11.15.a.m. and at 2.45.p.m.
48. 48 was active 3 times during the day, commencing at 2.50.p.m.
5. 5 was active at 4.30.p.m. firing salvos of 4 guns.
1. A Howitzer battery E. of BOIS DU BIEZ was active during the afternoon.
RITZ was shelled at 5.p.m.

II. OBJECTIVES ENGAGED.
48 by 110th Heavy Battery with time shrapnel.
Redoubt in S 10 b 6.1 by 30th Howitzer Battery (registration)
Red Houses in S 5 c 5.3 by 30th Howitzer Battery - 1 house set on fire.
Working party near Distillery by 110th Heavy Battery with time shrapnel - result good - party dispersed and stopped work.
Houses near PORT ARTHUR by 110th Heavy Battery at 3.30.p.m.
Houses in S 4 b 6.5 and S.4 b 6.3 by 2nd Siege Battery. Enemy trenches in S 5 c 3.5 and 3.0 registered.

III. INFORMATION.
Following "Redoubts" and works have been located:-
Redoubt S 10 d 5.5.   Earthworks S 11 c 2.5.
Much work done in S 10 b 5.5 and S 5 c 5.5.
Strongly sandbagged net work of trenches in S 10 b 5.0 - S 10 d 10.5
All houses in S 11 c have been loopholed and in some cases Chevaux de Frise has been put down in front of them.

Major R.A.
Brigade Major, Royal Artillery,
MEERUT DIVISION.

INTELLIGENCE SUMMARY UP TO 4.p.m. 8th MARCH 1915.

I. HOSTILE ACTIVITY seemed less marked to-day, except "Sniping"
which has increased to a marked extent along the RUE du BOIS.
52 52 shelled the RITZ about 12.40.p.m. and 2.p.m.
46 46 fired 3 rounds about 4.p.m.

II. OBJECTIVES ENGAGED.
Houses in S 11 a 7.8 by 30th Howitzer Battery
Red Observation House by 10th Heavy Battery.
Trenches in front of No 4 Picquet by 30th Howitzer Battery in reply
to heavy sniping from there
Registration of trenches proceeded with.

III. Germans in trenches have evidently been ordered to open with rifle
fire on our aeroplanes, a few shrapnel might help to keep this under.
The houses in S 5 a 5.6 to 8.9 and at road junction in S 11 a 7.8
have probably all a good view of PORT ARTHUR.
Houses in S 5 c 5.2 do not appear to be standing.
Reliable information has been received that the Germans are using
as a periscope in their front line of trenches, the battery
telescope described on page 148 of the "Handbook on the German
Army" as a tripod telescope with two arms connected by a hinge,
which can be turned upwards so as to see over a crest or extended
laterally on either side of a tree.
The information received goes to show that the Germans cover the
projecting part of this instrument with sacking or straw, where
it projects over the parapet. It would probably not project more
than three or four inches, and from the front would have the
appearance of the frayed end of a sandbag.
It appears possible that this battery telescope is being issued
to Infantry as well as gunners in the German Army.

Major R.A.
Brigade Major, Royal Artillery,
MEERUT DIVISION.

SECRET.
TIME TABLE.
FIRST PHASE.

Description of Gun.	Objective.	Time. Commence.	Cease.
15" Howitzer.	AUBERS and guns round AUBERS and POMMEREAU.	7.30 a.m.	
9.2" Howitzers.			
Three.	NEUVE CHAPELLE & outskirts.	7.30 a.m.	8.5 a.m.
One.	Railway triangle under orders of 1st Corps.	7.30 a.m.	as required.
6" Howitzers.	One battery. Ind.Corps. To shell selected spots.	7.30 a.m.	7.40 a.m.
18 pounders.	9 batteries. Ind. Corps. Wire-cutting.	7.30 a.m.	7.40 a.m.
-Ditto-	6 batteries, 4th Corps. Wire-cutting.	7.30 a.m.	7.40 a.m.
6" Howitzers.	4th Corps. Shell selected spots (5 batteries)	7.30 a.m.	7.40 a.m.
# 13 pounder. 1 baty.) 4.7" One section)	Three roads & trench running N.W. from BOIS du BIEZ.	7.35 a.m.	8.5 a.m.
4.7" One section.	"Gap" between Corps.	7.40 a.m.	8.5 a.m.
4.5" Howitzers.	Three batteries. 4th Corps. Enemy trenches.	7.40 a.m.	8.5 a.m.
-Ditto-	Three batteries. Ind. Corps. Enemy trenches & flank.	7.40 a.m.	8.5 a.m.
6" Howitzers.	Five batteries. 4th Corps. Enemy trenches.	7.40 a.m.	8.5 a.m.
-Ditto-	One battery, Ind. Corps. Enemy trenches.	7.40 a.m.	8.5 a.m.
18 pounders.	Twelve batteries. 4th Corps. Covering areas & flank.	7.40 a.m.	8.5 a.m.
-Ditto-	Eighteen batteries. Ind. Corps. Covering areas & flank.	7.40 a.m.	8.5 a.m.
13 pounders.	Three batteries. 4th Corps. Covering areas.	7.40 a.m.	8.5 a.m.
-Ditto-	Six batteries, 4th Corps. Belt of fire East.	7.40 a.m.	8.5 a.m.
4.7". One battery.	Trenches 4th Corps. Point 27.	7.55 a.m.	8.5 a.m.
	Roads & trench from BOIS du BIEZ.	8.5 a.m.	To end.

COUNTER BATTERIES.

6" B.L. Gun.	Counter batteries, AUBERS Ridge.	7.35 a.m.	
60 pr. Gun.	Counter batteries, under 1st. Corps. Area N. of Canal to BEAU PUITS,	7.35 a.m.	
4.7". 6 batteries.	Counter batteries.	7.30 a.m.	
4.7". 1 battery.	Counter battery.	8.5 a.m.	
One 6" Gun %) Armoured (Two 4.7" Guns.) Train ((% possibly) two 6" guns.)	AUBERS and guns near there.	7.35 a.m.	

Pack Artillery. 4th Corps. Two Sections. R.Column, one Section Left Column and to push forward.
Pack Artillery. Ind. Corps. Two guns close up in orchard, and both push forward.

SECRET.
SECOND PHASE.
8.5 a.m.

Description of gun.	Objective.	Time. Commence.	Cease.
15" Howitzer.	AUBERS and guns there.	8.5 a.m.	
9.2" Howitzers.	Two on NEUVE CHAPELLE.	8.5 a.m.	8.35 a.m.
	One on NEUVE CHAPELLE. and turn on to:-	8.5 a.m.	8.35 a.m.
	Two N.W.edge of BOIS du BIEZ	8.35 a.m.	9 a.m.
	One available for AUBERS, or continue at NEUVE CHAPELLE, if required.	8.35 a.m.	9 a.m.
6" Howitzers.	4th Corps. Lift.	8.5 a.m.	8.35 a.m.
-Ditto-	Indian Corps. Right flank.	8.5 a.m.	as required.
18 pounders.	4th Corps. Lift.	8.5 a.m.	8.35 a.m.
-Ditto-	Indian Corps. Lift.	8.5 a.m.	8.35 a.m.
-Ditto-	Indian Corps. One battery, on approaches of BOIS du BIEZ.	8.5 a.m.	8.35 a.m.
13 pounders.	4th Corps.	8.5 a.m.	8.35 a.m.
4.7". One battery.	BOIS du BIEZ.	8.5 a.m.	To end.

COUNTER BATTERIES.

4.7". Seven batteries.) Counter batteries, mainly
6" B.L., One battery.) AUBERS Ridge.

60 pr. Two batteries. Counter batteries under 1st
Corps. one covering area up
to ~~S~~ BEAU PUITS

One 6" gun) Armoured (
Two 4.7" guns) Train (AUBERS.   7.35 a.m.   To end.
         c/o Possibly 2/6" guns.

THIRD PHASE.

All 13 and 18 pounder batteries establish belt of fire
round front of the position.
One 4.7" battery - BOIS du BIEZ approaches.
Counter batteries)
Armoured Train   ) As before.

| 4.5" Howitzers | 4th Corps. Lift | 8.5 a.m | 8.35 a.m. |
| Ditto | Indian Corps. Lift | 8.5 a.m | As required |

AMMUNITION EXPENDED ON 10th., 11th., 12th and 13th MARCH 1915 by
LAHORE AND MEERUT DIVSNL. ARTILLERY

MEERUT.			LAHORE

10-3-15

18 pr.	Shrapnel	10134	18 pr. Shrapnel	5734
"	H.E.	307		
4.5	Lyddite	2550		
"	Shrapnel	386		
6"How.	Lyddite (heavy)	377		
6"Gun	Lyddite	92		
"	Shrapnel	83		
4.7	Lyddite	629		
"	Shrapnel	83		
"	C.P.	179		

11-3-15

18 pr.	Shrapnel	7364	18 pr. Shrapnel	3437
"	H.E.	12		
4.5	Lyddite	1037		
"	Shrapnel	364		
6"How.	Lyddite (light)	32		
"	" (heavy)	41		
"	Shrapnel	16		
6"gun	Lyddite	58		
"	Shrapnel	51		
4.7	Lyddite	430		
"	Shrapnel	176		
"	C.P.	27		

12-3-15

18 pr.	Shrapnel	3367	18 pr. Shrapnel	2614
"	H.E.	71		
4.5	Lyddite	870		
"	Shrapnel	109		
6"How.	Lyddite (light)	32		
"	" (heavy)	70		
"	Shrapnel	9		
6"Gun	Lyddite	76		
"	Shrapnel	46		
4.7	Lyddite	349		
"	Shrapnel	165		
"	C.P.	50		

Meerut Div.

C.R.A.

March 1915

www.ingramcontent.com/pod-product-compliance
Lightning Source LLC
Chambersburg PA
CBHW081436160426
43193CB00013B/2298